TENNIS
Origins and Mysteries

EARLIEST BOOK ILLUSTRATION OF TENNIS PLAY
From J. Sambucus, *Emblemata*, Antwerp, 1576

TENNIS
Origins and Mysteries

Malcolm D. Whitman

Dover Publications, Inc.
Mineola, New York

Bibliographical Note

This Dover edition, first published in 2004, is a slightly altered republication of *Tennis Origins and Mysteries*, originally published by The Derrydale Press, New York, in 1932. The Dover edition contains all of the author's text and all illustrations, but leaves out the Historical Bibliography by Robert W. Henderson, which comprised ninety-two pages of the original edition. The index has been corrected and its pages renumbered, and a few of the illustrations have been moved.

Library of Congress Cataloging-in-Publication Data

Whitman, Malcolm D. (Malcolm Douglas), b. 1877.
    Tennis : origins and mysteries / Malcolm D. Whitman.
        p. cm.
    "A slightly altered republication of Tennis origins and mysteries, originally published by the Derrydale Press, New York, in 1932"—T.p. verso.
    Includes index.
    ISBN 0-486-43357-9 (pbk.)
      1. Tennis—History. 2. Tennis—Bibliography. I. Title.

GV993.W5 2004
796.342'09—dc22

2004043648

Manufactured in the United States of America
Dover Publications, Inc., 31 East 2nd Street, Mineola, N.Y. 11501

Dedicated to

WILLIAM DANA ORCUTT

A LOVER OF LAWN TENNIS, LOYAL
FRIEND, ARTIST-PRINTER AND AUTHOR
WHO THROUGH THE MEDIUM OF THE
BOOK HAS TAUGHT ME EMANCIPATION
FROM THE TYRANNY OF THINGS

Tennis: Origins and Mysteries

TO THE lawn tennis enthusiasts of his own generation, the author of this volume needs no introduction. They saw Malcolm D. Whitman develop the game to a point beyond that of any of his contemporaries. During 1898, 1899 and 1900 they saw him win every important tournament, including the National Championship and the first International matches, and retire an undefeated champion.

Two years later came the second Davis Cup matches between Great Britain and the United States. On the English team were the two Dohertys, and the outstanding ability of those two great players was such that Mr. Whitman was virtually drafted for the American team. He played and won all his matches. In 1903 A. Wallis Myers of England wrote, " Whitman in his way is probably the greatest genius at the game that America has produced," and in 1916 in a published interview Tom Pettit, the famous professional who had seen all the great players and tournaments, said he was the greatest player up to that time. Those who saw Whitman in 1900 in the Davis Cup Matches at Longwood

[7]

defeat Gore, Champion of Great Britain the following year, will remember what a great advance in the previous art Whitman's strategy and strokes revealed. A reverse serve from high above his head employing the back instead of the face of the racquet, caused the ball not only to bound very high but at a wide and uncertain angle from its original direction. It was the development of this novel service, his unerring accuracy, and his ability to play in any part of the court that enabled him to establish his unique record, and retire an undefeated champion. The present generation may not be interested in past champions, but every generation is interested in the underlying characteristics that produce champions.

Malcolm D. Whitman is not only a player, but a student of lawn tennis, and his study did not cease when he retired from competition. During these years he has continued his research, each step confirming his early conviction that lawn tennis is an ideal form of outdoor sport, promoting alertness, endurance, self-control, and a wholesome condition of body and mind.

This volume is an outstanding contribution to the history of tennis and lawn tennis. It will be of absorbing interest to all those who have been players and followers of the game, but it will also become a reference book and valuable historical record. Its facts have been authenticated, many from original documents found frequently in remote places, often difficult of access. They have been obtained only after painstaking and exhaustive research generally found in the work of a professional historian. Yet there is nothing pedantic in the descriptive text. The reader's interest will be held from the first to the last page by the easy flow of language and skilful sequence of fact, humor and philosophy.

Of Malcolm D. Whitman's attitude toward the ideal of athletics, nothing could be more revealing than extracts from a reminder, prepared many years ago for his oldest son, and published in the *North American Review* for October, 1927:

" In any serious game of accomplishment, whether in business or in sport, when you feel that you are winning, when your instinct tells you that you have the game well in hand, be all the more cautious, all the more painstaking, all the more careful. Make assurance doubly sure. Let the prospect of your success quicken and enliven you to renewed effort.

" If you actually win, let it make you humble rather than proud. Never consider your crown of laurels, for too often it forms itself into a funeral wreath. The symbols of triumph can become the symbols of destruction in the twinkling of an eye.

" Remember that the difference between winning and losing, between success and failure, is but a hair's breadth. Leave no stone unturned. The best men of any given talent are those that struggle on till the last detail is properly done . . .

" Work hard at whatever you do. Work is the wine of the wise, the best antidote for boredom and the most wholesome recipe for a contented mind.

" So stick to your last to the last, my Son."

This letter to his son and the last chapter of this book reveal the author's real love for the game.

As a member of a family that first brought lawn tennis into the United States, and as one of the founders of the United States Lawn Tennis Association, I am glad to have the privilege of writing the introduction to this work.

Eugenius H. Outerbridge

CONTENTS

GRATEFUL acknowledgment is made to my beloved wife, LUCILLA DE VESCOVI WHITMAN, *Countess* ALFREDO JANNI, and the late *Dr.* PAOLO DE VECCHI, for interpretations of Old Italian and of Old French; to *Professor* PHILIP K. HITTI of Princeton for Arabic derivatives; to my former teacher, *Professor* GEORGE LYMAN KITTREDGE of Harvard, for English etymologies; to ROBERT W. HENDERSON of the New York Public Library for general assistance in research and bibliography; to JULIAN S. MYRICK for his generous coöperation in the collection of lawn tennis works; to WHITNEY WARREN for the rare volume of Scaino; to *Dr.* JOHN W. CUMMIN of Boston for rare clippings and references; to *Mrs.* T. SUFFERN TAILER for courtesy in lending the Marshall collection on court tennis; and to CLARENCE H. MACKAY for the use of his ideal court at Harbor Hill, and for the opportunity to study its records and illustrations.

ILLUSTRATIONS

ILLUSTRATIONS

TENNIS
Origins and Mysteries

SOMEWHERE over the rim of the world lies romance, and every human heart must yearn to find it: otherwise, life loses its savor and its song
The Island of Elcadar

I<small>N THE</small> work-a-day world of every-day affairs it is a great solace, once in a while, to go on a quest. If we can fold our tents quietly, and steal away to another land, it is a privilege and a delight. But often the coil of circumstance tightens about us so that all we can do is to let our minds take the wings of the morning, and fly out of the window to seek new adventure. This is the charm of books, the lode-star of a library, and our escape from the tyranny of things.

One evening, after a day of business worry, I sought refuge in the library, and found myself ruminating, more for diversion than anything else, among old records of tennis. Was it not this game, in all its forms, that had brought me so many hours of recreation and enjoyment? Was it not one of the oldest of games with a history extending back to the romantic time of the Crusaders? Deep in these reflections I made up my mind unconsciously to go on a pilgrimage among its dim, far-off and half-forgotten things.

In the fall of 1927, through the example and kindly influence of Henry Mortimer Brooks, one of the founders of The Racquet and Tennis Club of New York, I was persuaded to become interested in its library. The Club had a representative, though comparatively small list of books on lawn tennis, but a very complete collection of works on court tennis. It was this ancient game, played and favored by royalty, to which the later games owed so many of their traditions. Here was a rich source of information, a very rare collection of books and illustrations, modern and ancient references, the careful accumulation of more than twenty years. My desire for research was born anew. I studied the voluminous records, and determined to add to the Club's shelves all lawn-tennis works of note that were not already in its possession.

Robert W. Henderson, of the New York Public Library, had spent many years studying and cataloguing references to court tennis and lawn tennis, and I sought his assistance. Gradually we planned together a complete bibliography. A list of all works owned by The Racquet and Tennis Club on December 1, 1927, was prepared, and the collection of data began.

Then an important discovery beckoned further afield. In the course of my reading, and the bibliographical research of Mr. Henderson, we both began to suspect that the first edition of *The Major's Game,* the first book ever written on lawn tennis, had in some unaccountable way disappeared. It seemed incredible, but the more we compared notes the more convinced we became. Through an eminent English authority we were informed that the Queen's Club, of London, had a copy of the first book. It was described by E. B. Noel, an authority on court tennis, as "the first edition of a small book (no date) written by Major Wingfield, which I suppose is the earliest book on the game."[1]

A photostatic copy of the volume was then obtained, and an endorsement made by Julian Marshall, the greatest historian of tennis, appeared on one of its pages:

First Edition
November, 1874 (at earliest) see p. 31.
There is no copy in the Br. Museum.

Word came also from our English correspondent that "the first edition contains no date, but could not have been earlier than November, 1874."

All experts considered the Queen's Club copy the first edition. As such it was treasured by Julian Marshall, after his death by the late E. B. Noel, and later by the Queen's Club. Further search would have been abandoned if a brief note had not come to our attention.

In a London periodical[2] a letter written by one B. K. T. Smith, in answer to a query on the earliest work on lawn tennis, stated:

"As there appears to be no copy of Major Wingfield's pamphlet in the British Museum Library, and the first edition is mentioned only by hearsay in Foster's *Bibliography of*

---

[1] *National Review.* London, 1922. Vol. 80. p. 105.
[2] *Notes & Queries.* London, 1913. Ser. 11. Vol. 7. p. 506.

Lawn Tennis, the following particulars may be of interest. The contents consist of pp. 1–8, size 7 in. by 5 in."

And then other details of the book were given.

The Queen's Club copy contained thirty-five pages, while the copy referred to contained but eight. This little note led to a long search for the Smith copy. The story of that search is a tale of literary detective work, but it is too long to tell in these pages.

The Smith copy was secured. It is unquestionably an original first edition, and a book of extreme rarity. It is the only known copy which has been proved authentic to the satisfaction of experts. Its distinguishing characteristics are unmistakable, and they are pointed out for those who may be interested.[3]

Such a find was an inspiration, and led to deeper and deeper study. In the course of the work I was surprised again and again to discover how many unknown elements there were in lawn tennis that I had practised and studied so much from early boyhood, and in its predecessor, court tennis, that I have enjoyed in later years.

It all fired my imagination. I wanted to know the beginnings of everything—the origin of the game, its name, its terms, the racquet, the ball, the net, the method of scoring, and so on. The work became largely a search for origins, and while I do not profess to have discovered them all, for

---

[3] For Chart showing variations between the First, Second and Third Editions of the First Book on Lawn Tennis, *vide Appendix,* p. 152.

many still remain shrouded in mystery, I hope that what I have been able to find may prove of interest to the players of today.

Rainbows, origins, mysteries! Like the fugitive elements of beauty, which we can never wholly grasp, they lure us on and on. Some artful enemy may have placed them before me. Perhaps in this way mine enemies have persuaded me to write a book, and this is the beginning.

M. D. W.

New York, July, 1931

Chapter II

The Origin of the Word Tennis

THE NAME first applied to court tennis and later to lawn tennis is elusive and mysterious. Its origin, long said to be " unknown," is obscure. The word that began as *tenes* and ended as *tennis* has passed through twenty-four transformations, four variations of five letters, twelve of six letters, seven of seven letters, and one of eight letters.[1] It would almost seem as though the word changed its form to escape the etymologists.

As noted in the first English treatise on tennis, published anonymously in 1822 and later attributed to one R. Lukin:

" The unsettled state . . . of our orthography at that period (fifteenth century) forbids these varieties from becoming the ground-work of any speculations; nor does it seem at all expedient to lengthen out this note . . . by offering conjectures, which the reader may multiply at pleasure without much hope perhaps of arriving at the truth."[2]

---

[1] For Chart of various spellings and foreign equivalents, *vide Appendix*, p. 154.
[2] Lukin, R. *A Treatise on Tennis*. London, 1822. pp. 119–120.

There are certain derivations that have never been sub-stantiated, and may be disposed of at the outset to avoid confusion.

Lukin himself offers two theories not found elsewhere: one that tennis came from the French word *tente,* referring to a covered building in which the game was played, and another that it came from an old Norman word meaning "bound," this referring to the "cords or tendons" which were formerly wound around the hand to protect it in playing *jeu de paume* (tennis).

Other authors have claimed that tennis comes from the Latin word *teniludium,* meaning "play of tennis," and from a so-called Greek word *phennis.* The word *teniludium* is not endorsed by the leading Latin scholars, although *teniludus* and *teniludius* appear in a compilation of mediaeval expressions by a Dominican friar of Norfolk, England, in 1440.[8] There is not a shadow of Greek authority, however, for the word *phennis* as indicating tennis.

Other theories to be consigned to the realm of the imagination are: one, that tennis comes from the German *tanz,* the bounding or ricochet motion of the tennis ball, being a "tanz" or dance of the ball around the court; another that *tenne* is German for threshing floor, which was used at an early time for a primitive tennis court; another that tennis is old English for *tens,* and that the game is really double

---

[8] *The Promptorium Parvalorum.* Edited by A. L. Mayhew, London, 1908. (Early English Text Society, Extra Series No. 102) pp. 475, 830.

fives; another that *tence* (tenis) meant combat or batting to
and fro, and hence knocking a ball back and forth with a
racquet, it being said that *tence* is used with this meaning in
early English works; another that, as Tennyson and Deni-
son have been found to be the same originally, Saint Denis
was probably Saint Tennis, who became a patron saint, and
lent his name to the game.

We now come to the etymology that has been most generally accepted. In the opinion of J. J. Jusserand, former
Ambassador from France to the United States, the word
tennis in English comes from the French word *tenez*. His
argument is interesting, because it not only points out that
the game and all its terms were of French origin, but shows
that in early French days players tossed the racquet to determine who should have the serve, just as is done today:

" As for the French affiliation of lawn tennis, which has
not been known very long under its baptismal name, it is
not disputable nor disputed that it is derived from our
jeu de paume (tennis) . . . All its terms and methods suggest this origin . . . One gets the service in the French way,
at least the Royal Academy of Sciences said, speaking of
tennis, by throwing a racquet in the air with the exclamation
' droit' or 'noeud,' which corresponds to 'rough' or
' smooth ' in lawn tennis. The word *tennis* is itself of French
origin, and was written in primitive times *tenetz.*" [4]

----

[4] Jusserand, J. J. *Les Sports et Jeux d'Exercice dans l'Ancienne France.*
Paris, 1901. pp. 264–265.

Ambassador Jusserand, a profound scholar and a great student of early English literature, devoted much of his time to the history of sport, and his opinion should be given great weight. His conclusions are supported also by a great etymologist, W. W. Skeat. The first mention of tennis in the English language is contained in a communication by Gower to King Henry IV in 1399 or 1400. The important reference was at first quoted:

"Of the *tennés* to winne or lese a chace."

The discovery of an original manuscript, found among the effects of the Duke of Sutherland, revealed later that the original spelling was:

"Off the *tenetz* to winne or lese a chace."

From this discovery Professor Walter W. Skeat reaches this conclusion:

". . . I have found new evidence which goes far to settle it (the question) . . . The oldest spelling is actually *tenetz*. . . . There is thus an argument of the strongest kind, *viz.* from the oldest known spelling, that *tennis* was originally *tenez*, pronounced *tĕnéts*. All that remains is to suggest the sense. I suppose it meant 'take heed' or 'mark,' as an exclamation; if so, it is precisely the equivalent of the modern exclamation 'Play!' and if it was in frequent use at the beginning of a bout, it is easy to see how it was adopted as the actual name of the game." [5]

These conclusions have been further confirmed by another

---

[5] *Athenaeum.* London, 1896. Vol. 107. p. 447.

scholar in a later summary,[6] and by Jusserand himself in a later article.[7]

For a time an early Italian origin seemed plausible, for the first book on tennis, mentioned later, was written by an Italian, and the word itself first appeared in an Italian work, *Cronica di Firenze* (Chronicles of Florence), by Donato Velluti, who died in 1370. In this rare book, *tenes* first appears. The language of the description is very picturesque:

"Thomas of Lippaccio was an ecclesiastic, endowed with a benefice on the other side of the mountains (meaning beyond the Alps), beautiful in form, tall and courageous as a lion. He sold the benefice referred to, and came over here (to Florence), for there had arrived 500 French cavaliers that were the handsomest and finest set of people I ever saw, with plenty of money, all noblemen and great barons, among whom I saw one who was taller by a whole head and neck than any tall man, and his foot more than half an arm long. Almost all of them were killed at the defeat of Altopascio. He played all day with them at ball, and at this time was the beginning in these parts of playing at tenes."[8]

This is the only time the word is mentioned in Italian literature. It was never used before, and it does not appear

---

[6] Crawley, A. E. *Technique of Lawn Tennis.* London, 1923. pp. 17–26.

[7] Jusserand, J. J. *The School for Ambassadors.* 1925. pp. 217–223.

[8] Velluti, D. *Cronica di Firenze d'all anno M.CCC.,* in *Circa Fino M.CCC.-LXXX.* Firenze, 1731. p. 34. For original in old Italian, *vide Appendix,* p. 155.

again. Without doubt Velluti merely quoted the French knights, who brought the name and the game from over the mountains.

According to historical annotations of an enlarged edition of Velluti, published in Florence by G. C. Sansoni in 1914, the battle of Altopascio was fought on September 23, 1325, and the five hundred French knights, most of whom perished there, arrived in Florence on November 20, 1324. This date, therefore, may be regarded as the first appearance of the word *tennis* or its equivalent in any literature. It appears to be the very beginning. The notes also state that there is no other Italian evidence of this game "that was played with a ball and came from France."

The derivation from the French *tenez* or *tenetz* really rests upon the assumption that this expression was used by the French when they were about to strike the ball. Let us examine the evidence.

From 1324, and all through the fourteenth century thereafter, the word *tennis* in its various forms appears, but during this period no French literature records any mention of the players calling *tenez* or *tenetz* at the beginning of play. The first literature that makes such a suggestion does not appear in France but in England, and it does not appear until the seventeenth century. In 1617 a London lexicographer made a vast compilation in eleven languages, and this compilation contains the following:

"Tennis, play . . . *tenez* . . . which word the Frenchmen, the onely tennis players, use to speake when they strike the ball, at tennis." [9]

Here we have an Englishman, in compiling data from eleven languages, discovering a French expression that is not mentioned in French literature during a preceding period of more than two hundred and fifty years. Jusserand, after years of study, had to admit that attempts to discover a text giving the original French word actually used as an indispensable warning before playing had failed.[10] The *tenez* theorists then draw an analogy from the *Colloquies* of Erasmus, mentioned at length in Marshall, and the theory is adopted by Murray's *Oxford English Dictionary*.

The weight of authority favors the *tenez* theory, but the more the subject is studied the less satisfactory the theory becomes. It fails to convince a great many students of tennis history. The French had a universally adopted name for their game before *tenez* appeared in their literature. *Jeu de paume,* meaning tennis, was mentioned as early as 1200, and probably began to take form from 1150 to 1200. It is difficult to believe that an established name should have been changed from a mere exclamation at play. Furthermore, the transition from *tenez* or *tenetz* to *tennis* is not an easy one.

There is, however, another origin of the word for which considerable evidence has been discovered during the course

---

[9] Minsheu, J. *Ductor in Linguas. The Guide into the Tongues.* London, 1617. p. 486. *Vide Appendix,* p. 155.

[10] Jusserand, J. J. *The School for Ambassadors.* New York, 1925. p. 221.

of this search. It is offered as a stimulus to further study. During the primitive beginnings of tennis, in the latter part of the twelfth and the early part of the thirteenth century, French Crusaders brought into France from the Arabic speaking countries through Egypt certain words and forms. The Arabic word *rahat* meant "palm of the hand" or "shaped like a palm," and, according to eminent scholars, is the origin of our word *racquet*. Similarly, the Arabic word *hazard*, meaning literally "dice," was introduced into our language, and appears as a term in court tennis. These Crusaders visited, at different times, an ancient city on an island in the Delta of the Nile, described by the French archaeologists as La Ville de Tennis. This city was named "Tanis" by the Greeks, but earlier in the Arabic tongue it was called "Tinnīs," another spelling of the word *tennis*. It was a prosperous city, widely known for its manufacture of fine linens, and the *tissus de Tennis,* or light fabrics of tennis, became universally famous.

According to the most ancient manuscripts, the earliest word in French for ball was *esteuf*, a vulgar form of the word *étoffe,* meaning literally stuff, cloth, or fabric. The French word *balle* for ball was not introduced until the sixteenth century. The most authoritative French sources give a Latin derivation for *étoffe,* and define it as meaning tissues of silk, of wool, of cotton, and of other materials. Fabrics were called stuffs. The word so defined goes back to the thirteenth century, the very period in which we are

[29]

interested.[11] *Esteuf* is undoubtedly derived from the low Latin *stoffus* or *stofus*, and there is authority as early as 1356 to show that *stoffus*, or *esteuf* in the vernacular, was synonymous with *pila*, the Latin word for ball.[12]

In old French glossaries *esteuf* is more particularly defined as a ball for hand-ball play, especially for *jeu de paume* (tennis). The early balls were described as being made from pieces of light cloth rolled into a ball, and stitched with thread.[18]

We find woolen manufacturers in England in 1463 petitioning King Edward IV to prohibit the importation of " tenys balles." [14]

Sir Robert Dallington, commenting on the tennis of France in 1598, informs us:

" You observe here, that their Balles are of cloth, which fashion they have held this seven years: before which they were of lether like ours." [15]

There may have been an intermediate period in France when the balls were made of leather, but in the earliest times they were made of cloth or fabric.

An English poem indicates that at one time the balls in England were made of cotton fabric:

---

[11] Littré, E. *Dictionnaire de la Langue Française.* Paris, 1873. Vol. 2. p. 1522.
[12] Du Cange. *Glossarium Mediae et Infimae Latinitatis.* Paris, 1846. Vol. 6. p. 378.
[18] Gay, V. *Glossaire Archéologique.* Paris, 1887. Vol. I. p. 670
[14] *Rotuli Parliamentorum.* London, 1832. Vol. 5. p. 507.
[15] Dallington, Sir. *A Method for Trauell, Shewed by Taking the View of France. As it Stood in the Year of our Lord 1598.* p. 146.

The Origin of the Word "Tennis"

"My mistress is a Tennis-Ball
Composed of cotton fine."[16]

The travelers in Egypt from 1042 to 1226 mention the prosperous city of Tennis and its *tissus de tennis,* or light fabrics of tennis, although the city itself sank into the sea in 1226, and does not appear on any of the modern maps. It was well known, however, and described by the early geographers of Egypt.

We have, then, these facts from which to draw our conclusions: The ball preceded all games, and so preceded tennis even in its earliest forms. The very earliest balls were made of light fabric, and just about the time that tennis began, the best fabric was manufactured in a city that was always called by the French the city of Tennis. This was at the time of the Crusaders, and the French Crusaders visited the city of Tennis. These Crusaders introduced into France the Arabic word *rahat,* meaning "palm" or "shaped like a palm," which formed the basis of the name — game of the palm, or *jeu de paume* in French, and this became the origin of the word *racquet,* which took the place of the palm of the hand as the game progressed.

The Crusaders introduced into France and into the game of tennis another Arabic word, *hazard,* meaning literally at first "dice" and later "chance," as it does today. Then it would seem quite probable that the French Crusaders found in the city of Tennis balls made out of the fabrics manufac-

---

[16] *Merry Drollery Compleat.* London, 1691. p. 60.

tured there, and took them to France. If the balls of Tennis, or tennis balls, were the best that could be found, they may well have been adopted, and the name of the game may thus have come from the ball that preceded it, and was best suited for play. While this line of argument may not be conclusive, the historical records would appear to support it fully as much as they do the *tenez* theory.

Chapter III

The Origin of the Game of Tennis

ACCORDING to the purists, tennis can only mean real tennis — what we call court tennis in America. The exact beginning of the present game has not been and probably never can be definitely determined, because it has been a gradual evolution. For the purpose of discussion, however, its development may be divided into three periods: the embryonic, the formative, and the period after the game had become defined by the formation and publication of sets of rules or laws.

Ball play, or knocking a ball back and forth in the open and in various enclosures, was undoubtedly universal in earliest times. The country with the oldest language or historic records is in a position to maintain that it originated all ball play, because it can produce earlier records than other countries of playing with a ball in some form. But ball play in its earliest forms goes so far back that its origin is properly a subject for the archaeologist and the antiquarian.

The early forms of tennis undoubtedly came down to us through France, and it is justly said that tennis originated in France, even though France may have obtained some attributes of the game from older countries.

Major Walter Clopton Wingfield, the inventor of lawn tennis, in the third edition of his work *Sphairistiké* boldly proclaims a Greek and Latin origin for the game which he was adapting for out-of-doors on the lawns of England. He quotes a French poem to show that tennis was the most beautiful of all the games of skill invented by the Greeks. He then points out that it came down to us by way of the Latins, and continues:

" The Game of Tennis may be traced back to the days of the ancient Greeks, under the name of σφαιριστική, and the Athenians showed the estimation in which they held the game by according the rights of citizenship, and in erecting statues to Ariston of Carystius, a player who excelled at this exercise. It appears, from Pliny, that both the Greeks and Romans had *sphaeristeria,* or places appropriated to games of ball. Homer relates, in the vith Ode of the *Odyssey,* how white-armed Nausicaa, playing at the game with her handmaidens, hit the ball into the river. . .

" It was subsequently played by the Romans under the name of *Pila.* Horace, in the vth *Satire,* in which he describes his journey from Rome to Brundusium, tells how, at one of their halts, Maecenas, the energetic and fashionable man of the day, goes to play at Tennis while he and Virgil go to sleep. If Horace had played at Tennis, he would not have been so fat. . .

"It is probable that the game originally did not differ much from 'Fives.' It is stated that until the 15th century the ball was struck with the bare hand, whence, according to Pasquier, the French appellation of *Paume*. Afterwards the hand was protected by a stout glove, still occasionally used by the Basques, and a Racket was substituted about the commencement of the 16th century."

As far as proof of such origins is concerned, there is little that can be added to the above statement.

Earlier Egyptian, Persian, and Arabic origins have been suggested, and may serve as clues for fresh investigation and discovery. In an erudite article in *The Field,*[1] a well known personage of England, writing under the name of Antiquarius, gives Egyptian illustrations of ball play, and makes the statement that "the game must have come into France with the Saracen invasion, and the Greeks probably got a form of it straight from Persia or Egypt, very likely as early as 490 B.C." Another scholar and recent student of tennis adopts a similar view:

"Like all card and ball games, it does not appear doubtful that tennis came to us from the Orient, if not in the actual form at least in principle. If there is no absolute proof there are numerous arguments. In the fourth century of our era one finds in Persia a game called *tchigan,* which was played in a closed space with racquets four feet long; it cannot be confounded with polo, which was played in the same

---

[1] Antiquarius. In: *The Field.* London, 1927. Vol. 150. pp. 740–741.

epoch with a mallet and in the open air. This name of *tchigan* resembles closely that of ' chicane,' an old game in Languedoc. The word *tennis,* which has nothing English assuredly, for it has been used in the form of ténes or tenets in France, long before being in England, to designate tennis (*jeu de paume*), is of Arabic Origine if we believe Larousse, Littré, and the historian Maire." [2]

These accounts of the remote beginnings are stimulating, but an exhaustive survey recently made of the whole field of athletics of the ancient world reveals no proof, and tends to show that the ball play of the ancients lacked the competitive element and many other characteristics of tennis. [3] The illustrations in this work, taken from ancient vases and bas-reliefs, reveal a game played by the Greeks with a ball and a curved stick resembling hockey and other Egyptian and Grecian ball games, but nothing remotely resembling tennis.

We may turn to France, therefore, as the source of supply for most of our early information, and consider the formative period beginning with the earliest records in that country. Tennis was played in the open air, and with the bare hand, in the earliest days in France. During the fourteenth century, closed courts were built for the practice of the game, and these closed courts multiplied with amazing rapidity throughout the country, although the outdoor game

[2] Luze, A. de. *Le Jeu de Paume Jeu National Français.* In: *La Revue de Paris.* Paris, 1930. Année 37. T. 6. p. 349.

[3] Gardiner, E. N. *Athletics of the Ancient World.* Oxford, 1930. pp. 230–238.

EARLIEST PICTURE OF A GAME OF TENNIS, 1534
From Painting formerly owned by Julian Marshall

La Longue Paume des Champs Elises. *A Precursor of Lawn Tennis*

still continued. The game in France was called *jeu de paume* (game of the palm of the hand) and gradually the indoor game came to be known as *jeu de courte paume* (short tennis) and the outdoor game as *jeu de longue paume* (long tennis). Some maintain that the word *court* originated from the description of the indoor game. The outdoor game apparently passed into England, as we find there descriptions and illustrations of an outdoor game of "open or long tennis." This was undoubtedly copied directly from the game in France.

The origin of the racquet is very remote, and will be discussed later. Its adoption in tennis is not difficult to trace, however, and its evolution is shown in the accompanying illustrations. The game was first played with the bare hand, until a heavy glove was adopted for protection. Later, "cords and tendons were fastened around the hand in order to enable the player to give a greater impetus to the ball." [4] Panels or boards were then adopted, and still later handles were added. The instruments with handles were called "battoirs," and we find them described by Scaino, the author of the first book on tennis, as being of various shapes. The heads of the battoirs were later hollowed out and covered with parchment, and owing to this practice many precious manuscripts fell a prey to the battoir makers and tennis players of the time. Later, stringing took the place of parchment, and in this way the racquet in tennis was evolved. For

[4] Lukin, R. *A Treatise on Tennis.* London, 1822. pp. 2–3.

IN THE BEGINNING
La Paume, The Palm

TWELFTH CENTURY
The Glove

THIRTEENTH CENTURY
The Thong Binding

FOURTEENTH CENTURY
Battoir

FIFTEENTH CENTURY
Battoir

RACQUET OF 1555
Scaino

EVOLUTION OF THE RACQUET IN COURT TENNIS

RACQUET OF 1583
Nanteuil

RACQUET OF 1608
Rollo's

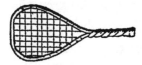

RACQUET OF 1675
Mitelli

RACQUET OF 1767
Garsault

MODERN RACQUET

EVOLUTION OF THE RACQUET IN COURT TENNIS

many years, however, tennis was played both ways, and there are old accounts of matches where players with racquets played opponents without racquets, and *vice versa.*

A reference to the drawings illustrating the evolution of the racquet will show the variations from time to time between diagonal stringing and the usual horizontal and perpendicular method that is used today. Racquets are still made with diagonal stringing in Europe. They are, perhaps, theoretically correct, but as a practical matter this method has a tendency to pull the frame out of shape. In any event, it is difficult to have such racquets restrung satisfactorily in America.

The illustrations also reveal the variations between the curved or spoon-shaped racquet and the straight racquet of today. Many players, especially of court tennis, believe that the curved or spoon-shaped racquet was devised in order to enable the player to impart a greater twist to the ball. The curved or spoon-shaped racquet, however, was probably adopted to enable the player to scoop the ball better out of the corners. This was the reason suggested by Scaino as long ago as 1555:

" The racket should be curved at the end, to enable one to return balls out of the corners." [5]

The indoor game was played in all kinds of enclosures, but the most colorful theory is that it originated in the ancient monastic cloisters:

---

[5] Marshall, J. *The Annals of Tennis.* London, 1878. p. 137.

JEV DE PAVME
XIVᵉ SIECLE

71

"Mr. Marshall (the great authority on tennis) has failed in all his efforts to discover the historic origin of the game which was so much the favourite of Henry IV of France that he got up at daybreak, the morning after St. Bartholomew, to finish a match (possibly in the court called that of the 'eleven thousand devils'); whose champion in 1427 was a woman; whose first record was a book written by an Italian in 1550 (*sic* 1555); the game which was rhymed by Rabelais and played by Benvenuto Cellini, and began to perish in France under the royal disfavour of the great Louis XIV, who hated all exercise except billiards. Nor has Mr. Marshall been able to find the origin of the English name 'tennis' — '*jeu de paume*' is clear enough, as the ball was first struck by the hand, — and where he failed in his antiquarianism we cannot hope to succeed. But we are surprised that he has taken no note of the tradition which almost proves its own truth, that the tennis-court, like the Eton fives-court, was the result of an accident of ground, and is, in fact, the copy of a monastery courtyard turned by the monks to the purpose of an improvised game. The two sides of the cloisters, the sloping roof, the 'tambour' (a jutting piece of wall), the 'grille,' with its very name, as the window where friends were to be seen, all forcibly bear the tradition out; and the tradition, say what we will, is very strong evidence. Be this as it may, the game was first a French one." [6]

---

[6] *New Book of Sports*. London, 1885. pp. 84–85.

This is a casual way of treating the important work of such an accurate scholar and historian as Marshall, especially as Marshall mentions the monastic references in early literature, and other scholars as late as 1924 have treated the subject as one of doubt:

"Another greatly disputed point is whether the court as we know it now or the courts of former times, of which plans or representations exist, were originally copied in one or more features from monastic buildings. The tradition that the 'grille' was the buttery hatch of a 'monastery,' the 'pent-house' part of the cloisters, and the 'galleries' cowsheds, may be purely legendary. It has never been satisfactorily proved or disproved." [7]

A very recent commentator favors a monastic origin, stating that the game became the game of kings "after having been the game of the bishops and the priests." [8]

The tennis court appears to have been a gradual evolution from rooms of various shapes. These rooms were in many types of structures — cathedrals, cloisters, chateaux, castles, moats, and even cowsheds. Though most of the earliest references are ecclesiastical, the history of the game is rich in its varied associations, all these various rooms having had an influence in its development.

Court tennis, or what the English purist would call tennis,

---

[7] Noel, E. B. and J. O. M. Clark. *A History of Tennis*. Oxford, 1924. Vol. I. p. 3.

[8] Luze, A. de. *Le Jeu de Paume Jeu National Français*. In: *La Revue de Paris*. Paris, 1930. Année 37. T. 6, p. 350.

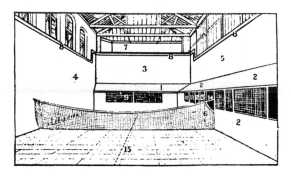

seen from hazard side

1, end pent-house; 2, side pent-house; 3, dedans high wall; 4, main wall; 5, side wall; 6, battery; 7, gallery for spectators; 8, play line; 9, dedans; 10, last gallery; 11, second gallery; 12, door; 13, first gallery; 14, line opening; 15, half-court line

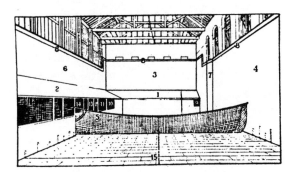

seen from service side

1, end pent-house; 2, side pent-house; 3, grille high wall; 4, main wall; 5, battery; 6, side wall; 7, tambour; 8, play line; 9, grille; 10, last gallery; 11, second gallery; 12, door; 13, first gallery; 14, line opening; 15, half-court line

INTERIOR OF MODERN TENNIS COURT

or real tennis, is not widely known. As Danzig writes in his recent volume:

"It is a game that is less read about than any other of the red-blooded sports. It is a game about the nature of which not one person in ten thousand in the United States has the slightest inkling. Of the 120,000,000 people who populate the country, not more than five thousandths of a per cent have seen it played, and less than half that number have a thorough understanding of it." [9]

According to the latest book on the subject:

"Including the private courts, the grand total of tennis courts in the world amount to 82, of which 60 are in use, and, of these, 29 are public and 31 private. This is striking evidence of the limited extent in which the game is played." [10]

To enable those unfamiliar with court tennis to visualize the game, two descriptive diagrams of a modern covered court are here given.

The earliest play of any game similar to tennis, of which there is a reliable record, is mentioned by Abbé Cochard, who states that ecclesiastical writers of the twelfth century reported the game as being played during their time. [11] About 1200 a bishop neglected evensong for the game of tennis. [12]

[9] Danzig, A. *The Racquet Game*. New York, 1930. p. 3.
[10] *British Sports and Sportsmen*. London, 1931. p. 175.
[11] *Mémoires de la Société Archéologique et Historique de l'Orléannais*. Paris, 1889. Vol. 28. p. 298.
[12] Vaublance, V. V. H. *La France au temps des Croisades*. Paris, 1847. Vol. 4. p. 261.

In 1245 the Archbishop of Rouen prohibited *jeu de paume* among the priests.[18]

In 1292 the *Rôle de la taille* of Paris, taken by order of Philippe le Bel, listed thirteen makers of balls for "palm play," this being one of the regular terms in Latin, French, and English synonymous with tennis. Paris at that time had only eight bookshops, so that the manufacture of tennis balls must have been quite an industry.

The astonishing part of the history of tennis now occurs. Without any question, the game passed to Great Britain in early times, but there is no satisfactory evidence of the approximate time. Noel and Clark say:

"Anything like the exact date of the introduction of tennis into England is impossible to say, but that it was well established in this country (England) towards the end of the fourteenth century is certain . . ."[14]

The earliest period mentioned in literature is in a description referring to the game in Britain:

"Although the life of Alexander III," says Mr. Fraser Tyler in his *Lives of Scottish Worthies,* cannot be estimated as the boundary between the authentic and the fabulous in Scottish history . . .

"For our special purpose in this paper it is a convenient starting-point, as during this king's reign (1249–1285) we

---

[18] Allemagne, H. d'. *Sports et Jeux d'Adresse.* Paris, 1903. p. 170.
[14] Noel, E. B. and J. O. M. Clark. *A History of Tennis.* Oxford, 1924. Vol. I. p. 4.

[44]

come upon the first authentic notices at home of the famous old game, which under various names, *paume, cach, tennis,* has been for so long a favourite pastime in this country.

"To France the world is indebted for tennis; but when the pastime began to spread abroad from the country of its origin into other lands is very uncertain. In Britain, at any rate, we can find no traces of it before the days of King Alexander.

"The mother of the Scottish king was Marie de Couci, daughter of that flower of chivalry, Enguerand of Picardy. It is supposed that the *jeu de paume* (tennis) was introduced into Scotland by the knights who came over from France in the train of the Queen; but, however this may be, whether they brought it over with them, or merely raised an existing game of 'fives' up to the scientific level of their own pastime, it is quite clear that tennis was a favourite game of king and courtiers during the too short reign of good King Alexander." [15]

Whether this period of transition to Britain is authentic is doubtful and difficult to determine, though we know the game was played in Scotland in early years.[16] The cavaliers of France apparently have the credit of spreading the game, carrying it to Great Britain as well as into Italy.

From the earliest contemporaneous records of tennis, the

---

[15] McGregor, R. *Tennis in Britain.* In: *Belgravia.* London, 1878. Vol. 37. pp. 68–74.

[16] Rogers, C. *Social Life in Scotland from Early and Recent Times.* Edinburgh, 1884. Vol. 2. p. 301.

epoch from the middle of the thirteenth century until 1592–1632, when the laws of the game were first formulated and later published, may be regarded as the formative period. The records are embroidered with interesting legends, quaint tales of royalty, and literary references.

Apparently, *jeu de paume* in the country was called *la bonde,* and in 1300 there is a play, *Miracle de Nostre Dame,* that refers to the game.[17]

In 1308, the Hôtel de Nesle, with all its appurtenances, was sold to Philippe le Bel. This château, with its tennis court, was where, in 1540, the famous Benvenuto Cellini played tennis.[18] In a description of Paris in early times, it is stated that the Hôtel de Nesle, with gárdens, vineyards, tennis court, etc., was sold to Philippe le Bel by Amandry de Nesle.[19] It is quite probable that this court in the Hôtel de Nesle was one of the most ancient in the world.

Eight years later, in 1316, King Louis X is reported to have died of a chill after playing tennis (*paume*) in a wood in Vincennes.

About 1368 the first walled-in courts appeared in France, Charles V of France having one at the Louvre, and another in the Hôtel de Beautreillis. At this particular time, the game came into extraordinary popularity. The public began to gamble with enormous stakes, and mountebanks of all

[17] Allemagne, H. R. d'. *Sports et Jeux d'Adresse.* Paris, 1903. p. 168.
[18] *Vide* quotation from Cellini's *Autobiography. Appendix,* p. 156.
[19] De la Force, P. *Description de Paris.* 1765. Vol. 8. p. 188.

kinds attended the matches, and imposed in one way or another on the spectators. The situation became so acute that in 1369 tennis was prohibited in Paris.

Between 1373 and 1384 the first references to tennis began to appear in England. In *Troylus and Creysede* we find the now famous phrase by Chaucer,

" But canstow playen racket to and fro."

This is the earliest mention of the racquet in English literature.

In 1388, in England, to promote archery, a law was passed providing that " servants and labourers shall have bows and arrows, and use the same the Sundays and Holydays, and leave all playing tennis, or football, and other games, etc." [20]

A similar law to promote archery had been passed in 1365, and this has frequently been quoted as prohibiting tennis, because it prohibited other games, but tennis in this law is not specifically mentioned.[21]

In 1397, an ordinance of the Provost of Paris informs us that " different artisans and others of the small people leave their work and their families during working hours to go for tennis playing, or bowling, or other games, throwing away not only their time, but their belongings." Similar laws were enacted in Holland in 1401 and 1413, prohibiting tennis play.

In 1437, at Yuletide, after his court had kept the festival of Perth in the Blackfriars Monastery, James I of Scotland is

---

[20] 12 Ric. II c6 1388.
[21] 39 Edw. III c23.

reported to have lost his life as an indirect result of his interest in tennis. As the original story goes, when conspirators entered to seize him, he escaped through a removable panel into a small vault, from which the door of a sewer led out of the castle. He had used this vault for tennis, and unfortunately had had the door walled up to keep the tennis balls from passing through. Thus blocked in his escape, he was captured by his enemies and assassinated.[22]

A year later, the famous woman champion, Mademoiselle Margot, appeared on the scene, the " Joan of Arc of Tennis." She defeated almost everyone, playing, according to the records, backhanded as well as forehanded. There is some argument among the commentators as to whether she played with or without a racquet, the game being played both ways at this time.

In 1435, the first poem on tennis was published. It was written by Charles d'Orléans, who likens life, with its trials and struggles, to the game of tennis. It is of great interest, because it is the earliest record yet found which suggests our present method of scoring by fifteens.[23]

About 1447 there was a controversy concerning tennis between the Bishop and the Mayor of Exeter. The Bishop accused the Mayor of allowing young people to play " atte tenys," by which " the walles of the saide cloistre have be

---

[22] . . . *A full lamentable cronycle of the dethe and false murdure of James Stewarde, Kyng of Scotys . . . From a manuscript written MCCCCXL.* Glasgow, 1818. p. 16.
[23] For poem *vide Appendix*, p. 157.

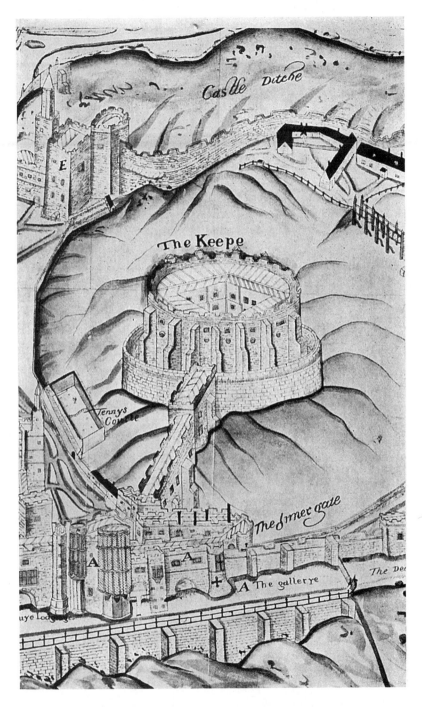

FIRST COURT IN ENGLAND AT WINDSOR CASTLE
From Original Manuscript in British Museum

defowled and the glas wyndowes all to brost . . ." And the Mayor retorted that the Bishop's officers were bootleggers of " ale and wyne," which they sold higher " than hit aughte to be solde . . ." [24] This tale has a modern flavor.

About 1450, also, a reference to tennis appears in one of the early miracle plays, *Secunda Pastorum*. The third shepherd advises his friend to " go to the tenys." [25]

The accompanying illustration, from a manuscript now in the British Museum, shows an early if not the first tennis court in England. It was at Windsor Castle, in 1505, that Philip, Archduke of Austria and King of Castile, played a match with the Marquis of Dorset, attached to the court of Henry VII of England. The account suggests the grandeur of the occasion:

" King Philip subsequently took his journey toward Windsor Castle, where the king lay: and five miles from Windsor the Prince of Wales, accompanied with five earls and divers lords and knights, and other to the number of five hundred persons gorgeously apparelled, received him after the most honorable fashion."

The following is the contemporary narrative of the King's reception and entertainment:

" Memorandum that the XXXI of January wch was one of a Sattordaye in the yeare of our Lord 1505 and the 21

---

[24] Shillingford, J. *Letters and Papers of John Shillingford, Mayor of Exeter 1447–50.* Westminster, 1871. pp. 91–2, 101.

[25] *The Townley Mysteries.* London, 1836. p. 116. (Surtees Society Publications, Vol. 3.)

yeare of our Soveraigne Lord Kynge H. 7, his Highness re-
ceaved the kynge of Casteelle at his castell of Windesore in
manore as followethe: .. The Sattordaye the 7 of ffeb-
ruary . . . Both kyngs went to the tennys playe and in the
upper gallery theare was Layd ij Cushenes of Clothe of
gold for the ij Kings . . . wheare played my Lord marques,
the Lord Howard and two other knights together, and
aftere the kynge of Casteele had seene them play a whylle,
he made partye wth the Lord Marques of Dorset the kynge
Lookynge one them, but the kyng of Casteele played w^th
the Rackete and gave the Lord Marques xv. and after that
he had pled his pleasure and arayed him selfe agene it was
almoste nighte, and so bothe kyngs Retorned agayne to their
Lodginges." [26]

A recent work states that this court existed during the
fifteenth century, and indicates that it was the earliest court
in England.[27] No illustrations of any earlier court in England
are to be found in the British Museum.

In 1508, tennis arrived at Oxford, four men being arrested
for " keeping tennysplayes." It was in the same year that
Count Baldassare Castiglione, in the first draft of his work
on life at the Court of Urbino, refers to tennis as an ideal
all-round exercise for a courtier. His work, originally published in 1528, was later translated into Spanish, French,
and English. Sir Thomas Hoby, a traveler in Italy and at

[26] Tighe, R. R., and Davis, J. E. *Annals of Windsor*. London, 1853. Vol. 2.
pp. 434–441.
[27] *British Sports and Sportsmen*. London, 1931. p. 173.

Tennis Player with Racquet, 1583

one time British Ambassador to France, gives this description from his commentary:

" Also it is a noble exercise, and meete for one living in Court to play at Tenise, where the disposition of the bodie, the quicknes and nimblenesse of everie member is much perceived, and almost whatsoever a man can see in all other exercises." [28]

Apparently the game was not only regarded as eminently fitting for a gentleman and a courtier, but, long after the racquet came into use, it was considered more elegant to play with the hand. In 1524, we find, in the *Colloquies* of Erasmus, a statement showing that at that late date they still played with the hand:

Imo reticulum piscatoribus relinquamus elegentius est palma uti (" Let's leave the net-covered instrument to the fishermen; it is more elegant to use the hand)." [29]

In 1533, Rabelais came upon the scene of tennis literature. Rhymed by Rabelais is a catching phrase often quoted, but what he rhymed is so little known that it may bear repeating, especially as this description shows how tennis was regarded by the students of the time. In describing Pantagruel's travels, Rabelais relates:

" Going from Bourges, he came to Orleans, where he found store of swaggering Scholars that made him great entertain-

---

[28] Castiglione, B. *The Book of the Courtier*. Done into English by Sir Thomas Hoby, 1561. New York, 1928. p. 42.
[29] Erasmus, D. *Colloquia Familiaria*. Ulmae, 1712. p. 50.

ment at his coming, and with whom he learned to play at tennis so well, that he was a Master at that game; for the Students of the said place make a prime exercise of it. . .

"As for breaking his head with over-much study, he had an especial care not to do it in any case, for feare of spoiling his eyes; which he the rather observed, for that it was told him by one of his teachers (there called Regents) that the paine of the eyes was the most hurtful thing of any to the sight: for this cause when he one day was made a Licentiate, or Graduate in law, one of the Scholars of his acquaintance, who of learning had not much more than his burthen, though in stead of that he could dance very well, and play at tennis, made the blason and device of the Licentiates in the said University, saying:

"'So you have in your hand a racket,
    A tennis-ball in your cod-placket,
    A Pandect law in your caps tippet,
    And that you have the skill to trip it
    In a low dance, you will b' allow'd
    The grant of the Licentiates hood.'" [80]

In 1555, in Venice, the first book on tennis was published. It is mentioned in some detail in a later chapter.

In 1564, a learned Hungarian and court physician to King Maximilian, published his *Emblemata*, in which the first

---

[80] Rabelais, F. *Gargantua and Pantagruel*. Translated into English by Sir Thomas Urquhart and Peter Le Motteux. London, 1900. p. 217.

book illustration of tennis is to be found. Under the picture, which is shown as the frontispiece, there is a satirical poem in Latin, the poet personifying and addressing the ball. Tennis had just come into fashion among the aristocrats of Vienna. As a physician, Dr. Sambucus could not see the reason for playing indoors, when the open fields were available. Apparently he made no allowance for those who have to dwell in cities. He objected also to the stylish clothes of the dandies of the time as interfering with the free movement of the body.

Shortly thereafter, tennis began to be mentioned in plays. In addition to Shakespeare's *Henry V,* the Webster play of *The Duchess of Malfi,* printed in 1623 and probably acted in 1616, has an enlightening comment on a cardinal. It illustrates how tennis was regarded at the time.

"... They say he's a brave fellow. Will play his five thousand crowns at tennis, dance, Court ladies, and one that hath fought single combats." [81]

The popularity of tennis in the early part of the seventeenth century is evidenced by the fact that in 1641 the ladies wore their hair *en racquettes,* that is, in cross or plaited bands. Catherine de' Medici was among those who dressed their hair in this manner.

In May, 1641, one R. Frissart, describing himself as " the oldest of living tennis players, and, unless his vanity de-

---

[81] Webster, J. *The Duchess of Malfi.* In: Webster & Tourneur. With an introduction and notes by John Addington Symonds. London, 1888. p. 318. (The Mermaid Series.)

ceived him, the steadiest," published, with an adulatory ad-
dress to Cardinal Richelieu, a pamphlet on the game in
Latin, illustrating in an interesting discourse many of the
technical points of tennis as it was then played.[32]

The rules or laws of tennis were written and printed, as
more fully described later, between 1592 and 1632. If the
establishment of rules or laws may be accepted as the true
origin of a game, tennis, that is, court tennis as we understand it today, may be said to have been born at this period,
though its earlier forms existed centuries before.

---

[32] Marshall, J. *Annals of Tennis.* London, 1878. pp. 25–30.

Chapter IV

The Origin of Court Tennis in America

ACCORDING to the most recent histories of tennis, and the latest accounts in various encyclopaedias, the game of tennis was first played in America in the city of Boston in 1876. In the fall of that year a private court was opened on Buckingham Street by Hollis Hunnewell and Nathaniel Thayer, and a professional player was brought over from Oxford to take charge. Noel and Clark refer to it:

" The old court at Boston has now disappeared, but, as the first in America, it will always be a notable memory." [1]

In the course of this present search, however, references have been found which reveal the fact that the game was played in America much earlier. Working backward in point of time, we find that in 1766 James Rivington imported battledores and shuttlecocks, cricket balls, pillets, best racquets for tennis and fives, backgammon tables with men, boxes, and dice." [2]

[1] Noel, E. B., and J. O. M. Clark. *A History of Tennis.* Oxford, 1924. Vol. I. p. 79.
[2] Singleton, E. *Social New York under the Georges.* New York, 1902. p. 265.

Earlier, in 1763, " a very fine Tennis Court or Five-Alley " in New York City was offered for sale at public auction. Unfortunately there is no description of this court other than that contained in the advertisement shown in the illustration.

But the earliest and most conclusive evidence discovered is contained in a lengthy and ancient document now on file

To be Sold at Publick Vendue on Friday, 29th of April, on the Premises, or at private Sale any Time before, A Good new commodious Dwelling House and Lot of Ground, together with another Lot adjoining, both Lots at 6£. per Annum Quit Rent to the Corporation. The House has five Fire-places, and an excellent Cellar Kitchen : It has all the Conveniences fit for a Tavern, is now kept as such by the Owner Martin Pendergraft, at the Sign of the Hurlers ; has a very fine Tennis-Court, or Five-Alley, and lies between the New-Gaol and Fresh Water Hill.—A good Title will be given by   MARTIN PENDERGRAST.

ADVERTISEMENT IN *New York Gazette* (*Weyman's*), April 4, 1763

in the Stad Huys (City Hall) in the city of Amsterdam, in Holland. According to this document, Peter Stuyvesant, Governor of New York, on September 30, 1659, proclaimed that Wednesday the fifteenth of October in the same year should be a day for general fasting and prayer. The document is of unusual interest because it proves that tennis must have been played quite extensively in America prior to 1659. It throws light also on the religious attitude of some of our early settlers.

TENNIS MASTER
An Engraving by C. Monath, Nuremberg, 1650

TENNIS MASTER

From Early German Illustration, 1723

It is the skill and art of how to judge the ball,
A pastime of a kind most pleasing to the great,
But though it be held high in courtly estimate
A student too the game may choose withal,
If he do not its exercise so use
That in its very practice his best time he lose.

(TRANSLATION)

"Although the most merciful God . . . daily gives us abundant cause to proclaim His praise . . . Yet . . . hath visited many and divers inhabitants of the Province . . . with painful and long, lingering sickness, but, moreover, also, that His kindled anger and uplifted hand threaten with many and divers punishments, especially with a devastating Indian war, which is no other than a just punishment and visitation of our God for our enormous sins . . . therefore, we have considered it most necessary . . . to proclaim Wednesday the 15th October of the current year, a day of Universal Fasting and Prayer . . . solemnly to call on the Lord's name that it may please His Divine Majesty to remove from our road His just plagues, wherewith we are already stricken, and to divert His rod, which flourishes over us, and to pour down His wrath on the Heathen who know not His name. . .

"In order that it may be the better put into practice, we interdict and forbid, during divine service on the day aforesaid, all exercise and games of tennis, ball-playing, hunting, fishing, ploughing and sowing, and moreover, all other unlawful practices, such as dice . . . on pain of the corporeal correction and punishment thereunto already affixed."

It is to be remembered that tennis was at its height in Europe at this period. The game must have been played in America prior to the time of Governor Stuyvesant's proclamation, otherwise he would not have put it at the head of the list of all games to be prohibited on the day appointed for universal fasting and prayer. The proclamation in many respects resembles the restrictive enactments passed in the early days in France and England, and in Holland as well. It is surprising, therefore, that earlier references to tennis in America have not been brought to light before this time.

Chapter V

The Origin of "Love" in Scoring

THE PLAYERS of today who call the scores so glibly may be surprised to know that they speak a language which has been a puzzle for centuries. While the use of "fifteen" in tennis scoring still remains obscure, as pointed out later, the use of the word *love* is the great mystery. It is so mysterious that it is not discussed in an authoritative way by any of the historians. Although of comparatively recent origin, for the word has no foreign equivalent and was first used by the English, no one really knows why it was used, nor exactly when it was first used. Only a few casual references or bold assertions appear in tennis literature. For example, one author states didactically that the word comes from an old Scotch word *luff*, meaning "nothing," and this has been repeatedly quoted.[1] According to the authorities, however, no such word has been used at any time in the Scotch language. Most writers who mention "love" at all, dismiss it with a hopeless gesture. There are, however, certain theories, legendary and otherwise, that are interesting to consider.

One of these, which has come down by word of mouth for many years, is to the effect that the French, the earliest

[1] Monckton, O. P. *Pastimes in Times Past*. London, 1913. p. 205.

exponents of court tennis, in marking up a zero to indicate no score, wrote the figure in an elliptical form. This figure often had the appearance of an egg, and so the French called it *l'oeuf* (the egg). It has been said that when the English learned the game from the French they heard the French calling *l'oeuf* for no score, and this sounded to them like the word *love,* so they called it "love," and have continued to do so ever since.

To support this theory an analogy is drawn from the game of cricket. In that game the zero or "O" placed against the batsman's name in the scoring sheet when he fails to score is used to designate "nothing," and this score for a long time has been called "the duck's egg" or "duck egg." [2] There are cricketers today who say they used to call it "the duck" for short.

In a glossary of words and phrases in a history of the game of cricket, the duck's egg is defined as a term relating to "the cipher, so frequently appended to an unfortunate batsman's name." A quaint rhyme is quoted to illustrate the point:

> And when eleven are matched against eleven,
> And wrestle hard the mastery to gain,
> Who tops the score is in the seventh heaven,
> Who lays an *egg,* in an abyss of pain.
>
> — M. K. Brodie, 1865 [3]

---

[2] Murray, J. A. H. *New English Dictionary.* Oxford, 1897. Vol. 3. Pt. I. p. 702.   [3] Box, C. *English Game of Cricket.* London, 1877. p. 449.

An analogy is also drawn from the slang expression "goose egg" as applied in other games. It is said that this expression originated in the United States, *The New York Times* being referred to as giving the following description of a baseball game in 1886:

"The New York players presented the Boston men with nine unpalatable goose eggs in their (baseball) contest on the Polo Grounds yesterday." [4]

Another "egg" enthusiast also calls attention to an old French proverb, which is to be found with a quaint translation in an ancient dictionary:

> "*Un oeuf n'est rien; deux font grand bien;*
> *trois c'est assez; quatre c'est tort; cinq*
> *c'est la mort: Pro.*"

> "One egge is none, two somewhat, three enow;
> foure be too much, five give a deadly blow." [5]

The difficulty with the argument is that in court tennis the points in each game are not placed upon a score board today, and there is only a shadow of evidence to indicate that they were ever so placed in times past. Furthermore, the authority for the French calling out "*l'oeuf*" to indicate "no score" is as legendary as the theory itself.

But the nothingness of love in tennis, so to speak, appears to act as a continual stimulant to the imagination. It is sur-

---

[4] Murray, J. A. H. *New English Dictionary.* Oxford, 1897. Vol. 4. p. 300.
[5] Cotgrave, R. *A Dictionarie of the French and English Tongues.* London, 1611. Also 1632 edition with English-French addenda.

prising that some brilliant commentator has not made use of the ancient story of the two ladies who fell so much in love with the Duc de Nemours that they often left church to watch him play tennis. Fanciful theories are being suggested from time to time, but usually in conversations, the authors not having sufficient faith in their theories to commit them to writing. For example, one scholar recently suggested that the word *love* had always been associated with games by the ancient Greeks, and that this thought had undoubtedly percolated through the centuries, and so was used in connection with tennis. To support this idea he offered a translation of a Greek poem written in 150 B.C.:

Love's Tennis

Love and Desire play the set,
　My heart's the flying ball.
To Heliodora, cross the net,
　They send it, rise and fall.

Be heedful, sweetest; watch thy art
　Nor mock me in my need.
To miss the stroke and lose my heart,
　That were a fault indeed.

A. P. v. 214.[6]

This led to further study, and another translation of the same poem by another scholar was found:

---

[6] *The Complete Poems of Meleager of Gadara.* Translated from the Greek by F. A. Wright. London, 1924. p. 111.

[62]

The Origin of "Love" in Scoring

Love the Ball Player

"I cherish Love, the ball player; he throws to you, Heliodora, the heart which trembles in me.

"Let Desire come, too, as a player; but if you place me away from you I will not endure this breach of the rules of the palaestra!" [7]

How such references can support the theory of the use of *love* in scoring is difficult to comprehend, but they illustrate at least the eagerness to find an answer, an urge that has led to a new theory. It is offered with a good deal of deference, because it appears so obvious, and it is so easy, in studies of this kind, to make an error. The idea that has developed during the course of this search is based on the earliest history of the word itself.

The use of the word *love* to suggest "nothing" is as old as the English language. In the year 971 we find the equivalent of the expression "neither for love nor money," "ne for feu, ne for nanes mannes lufou." [8] Similar expressions have been in common use for centuries. Later, by an easy antithesis, there developed the expression in competitive games "to play for love," meaning "to play for nothing," as contrasted with playing for money. Similarly, a labor of love, though originally meaning a labor one delights in,

---

[7] *The Poems of Meleager of Gadara.* Translated by Richard Aldington. London, 1930. p. 16. *Love the Ball Player.*

[8] Blickling Homilies, 971. In: Murray, J. A. H. *A New English Dictionary.* Oxford, 1908. Vol. 6. Pt. I. p. 464.

came to mean a labor done for favor, for love, or for nothing. In earlier Latin, also, we find a similar development. *Gratiis,* shortened later to *gratis,* meant literally "for favor" or "love," but it came to mean in Latin just what it now means in English, "gratis," "for nothing."

Down through the centuries similar expressions appear. The first application of the phrase to a game was in 1678, Samuel Butler in *Hudibras* saying, "and play for love and money too." [9]

In 1725, Bailey, in translating Erasmus' famous dialogue on tennis, treats nothing as love: "I have seen those lose the game that had so many for love." [10]

Similarly we find, in 1736, an old saying used by shop-keepers to encourage their customers to look at their wares, "See for love and buy for money." [11] And in 1742 the phrase is used by Hoyle in his rules on the game of whist. [12]

"To play for love in competitive games meant to play for nothing." [13]

Modern writers use the expression in precisely the same way:

"The old literature of tennis abounds in facts and anecdotes which seem to prove that the game was hardly ever played for love. The stakes were placed 'under the cord,'

[9] Butler, S. *Hudibras.* London, 1678. Part III. Canto I. line 1007.
[10] Erasmus, D. *Familiar Colloquies.* London, 1733. p. 39.
[11] Bailey, N. *Dictionarium Britannicum.* London, 1736.
[12] Hoyle. *Whist,* 1742. Vol. I. p. 13.
[13] Murray, J. A. H. *New English Dictionary.* Oxford, 1903. Vol. 6. Pt. I. p. 465.

a position which reminds one of the old cricket fashion of putting sovereigns on the stumps. . ."[14]

It is quite usual to say, "Let's play for love," when we mean to play for nothing, and in view of the antiquity of this expression it would seem most natural for the English to have used the word to indicate no score when they first began to play the game.

---

[14] Crawley, A. E. *The Field*. London, 1913. Vol. 122. p. 301.

Chapter VI

The Mystery of "Fifteen" in Scoring

THERE HAS always been an atmosphere of mystery about certain numbers. In ancient days, three and seven were regarded as lucky. Today, in mathematics, the curious characteristics of nine form the basis of a short method of calculation. All numbers that are multiples of nine have digits that add up to multiples of nine, and there are other interesting combinations.

In tennis, from the earliest times, the number fifteen has been the unit of calculation. Few tennis players of today fully appreciate the antiquity and the obscurity of their method of scoring, for references to the subject are scattered, appearing in rare and remote volumes. They are in different languages, modern and ancient.

To begin at the beginning, we find the first indication of scoring by fifteens in a French ballad[1] composed by Charles d'Orléans in 1435, while he was imprisoned in Wingfield Castle, in England. This ballad, likening life with its trials and struggles to the game of tennis, refers to *quarante cinq,* the original expression in French for *quarante,* just as in

---

[1] *Vide Appendix,* p. 157.

early days in England forty-five was the original expression for forty in tennis scoring.

The next mention of scoring by fifteens occurs in the account mentioned earlier of the match between King Philip of Castile and the Marquis of Dorset, played at Windsor Castle in 1505, the King playing with a " racket," and giving the Marquis a handicap of " XV."

Another reference occurs about 1522, and is in Latin. In a dialogue between two tennis players this expression occurs: *Vicimus triginta, vicimus quadraginta quinque* (" We are winning thirty, we are winning forty-five ").[2] This clearly indicates that scoring by fifteen was already well established.

The next reference is of great importance. It is the first discussion of the subject in any language, and it appears in a work that is so rare and of such interest as to deserve particular comment.

Lord Alfonso da Este, Prince of Ferrara, later made Duke of Ferrara, the grandson of Alfonso I and the famous Lucrezia Borgia, was a man of commanding physique, and deeply interested in various sports. While watching a tennis match he raised a question about a point in the game, and one of his followers, a very learned man, attempted to answer the question. It was this episode that led Antonio Scaino da Salo, a priest and doctor of theology, to write the first book in the world on tennis. It was published in Venice in 1555, and contains this dedication:

---

[2] Erasmus, D. *Colloquia Familiaria.* Ulmae, 1712. p. 52.

Tennis: Origins and Mysteries

DEDICATED TO THE

MOST ILLUSTRIOUS AND MOST EXCELLENT

LORD,

THE LORD ALFONSO DA ESTE PRINCE OF FERRARA

Venice, 18 August 1555

The work, *Tratta del Giuoco della Palla,* is a learned treatise on all the ball games that were played up to that period, and contains a full description of tennis (*palla della corda*). It is of unusual historic interest, not only because it is the first work but also because it contains illustrated diagrams of the different implements used in different games, including an accurate diagram of a court built by Francis I of France at the Louvre. It is strange that the first book about tennis, which originated in France, should have been written by an Italian and published in Italy. Scaino's book is referred to repeatedly in the historical records of France and of the city of Paris, and was undoubtedly regarded as a work of great authority.

Scaino informs us that even in his time each stroke won scored fifteen for the winner: that is, for the first, fifteen; for the second, thirty; for the third, forty-five; or at one (*a una*), meaning only one stroke necessary to win; and at two (*a due*), when the game is " set " at two strokes to be gained for winning. The term *a una* is now obsolete, but *a due* is still preserved in the French expression *à deux,* and in the English equivalent " deuce." The term " advantage,"

[68]

EARLY VENETIAN GAME ANALOGOUS TO TENNIS. From Painting by Gabriele Bella, c.1750

in Italian *vantaggio*, like *avantage* in French, was also used at that time. The only change that has taken place during the course of centuries has been the contraction from forty-five to forty, a change undoubtedly made merely for the sake of brevity and ease in calling the score.

In approaching the mysterious counting by fifteen, Scaino states at the very outset that after most diligent search he has been unable to find any literature, ancient or modern, on the subject. He then offers what appears to be his own explanation of why the number fifteen was adopted as the unit of counting.

His explanation is difficult to understand, and has not been clearly explained by the commentators. The old Italian of the fifteenth century is usually simple and clear, but Scaino's work is in the complicated and involved style of the middle of the sixteenth century. It is necessary to consider his whole treatise in order to grasp his idea of why fifteen was adopted.

Apparently, the number of points to a game in Scaino's time was exactly as it is today. There were three types of game generally referred to by tennis players of the time. These three types of game were called the simple, the double, and the triple. The simple game was where points were won and lost on both sides. The double game was where one player won four consecutive points, or, in other words, a love game. The triple game, however, was something quite unusual. Here, one player with three points against him, or, in the language of today, love forty, won out by scoring five consecutive points. It was supposed to be a great accomplishment for a player to win a triple game, and he was said to earn thereby " the three degrees of honor and reward."

The triple game apparently was quite prominent in the terminology of the time. Scaino's idea was that in scoring in tennis the players wanted to use some symbol that would embody or suggest fully the distinguishing attributes of the triple game. These were three and five, and fifteen was adopted as the symbol of counting because it was the first numeral that embodied three and five, containing five three times and three five times.

For some curious reason the commentators have given very little weight to Scaino's explanation, although it is just as plausible as other theories that have been advanced. Apparently, in other games in Italy at the time, the same method of counting by fifteen was used, even in the ancient game of *rebot,* that is still played in the Basque provinces.[3]

Further study may eventually prove that Scaino's theory is correct, imaginative as it may at first appear. It must be remembered in this connection that all symbols are products of the imagination, and that often a symbol is adopted through a mere suggestion or through a mere association of ideas. In the writer's judgment, there is no evidence to show that Scaino's theory, the first and oldest, is incorrect, although scholars hitherto have given it little or no weight.

Another interesting discussion appears twenty-four years

[3] Blazy, E. *La Pelote Basque.* Bayonne, 1929. p. 217.

later in an unusual French booklet of which there is said to be but one copy in existence. This, bearing the date of 1579, has an odd history. The author's full name does not appear in its pages. Its substance has been absorbed in later volumes without comment and without any account of its distinguished author. As a matter of fact, it was written by one Jean Gosselin, and is the first treatise on the subject in French literature. Gosselin was a great scholar, an astrologer, and a mathematician. He was Royal Librarian under four of the kings of France. One of his letters reveals that the Royal Library was originally at Fontainebleau, but that at the command of Charles IX he transferred it to Paris, where it became the *Bibliothèque Nationale*.[4] Jean Gosselin guarded the rare treasures of the Royal Library for many years, and his efforts and writings are largely responsible for the preservation of this famous library. It is said that he attained an age of almost a hundred years, and that he met his death by falling from his armchair into the open fire before which he had been sitting. He was too feeble to extricate himself.

There appears to be but one copy of Gosselin's original treatise, and it is in the *Bibliothèque Nationale*. The rules and laws of tennis were formulated by Forbet, Sr., a *maitre paumier* in 1592, and were printed in 1599 in Paris by Sevestre, and reprinted with revisions by Hulpeau in 1632.

---

4 Franklin, A. *Précis de l'Histoire de la Bibliothèque du Roi Aujourd'hui. Bibliothèque Nationale.* Paris, 1875. p. 86.

Gosselin's article and all these rules and laws of tennis were bound together in one volume, and this has in a sense been treated as one book. Possibly it is for this reason that the story of Jean Gosselin is not told by any of the historians of tennis.

Gosselin's treatise is entitled *Declaration de Deux Doubtes qui se trouvent en comptant dans le Jeu de Paume* (" Statement of two doubtful points that are found in counting in the game of tennis "). It is dedicated to François, Marquis D'O, and is subscribed simply *Gosselin, Garde du Libraire du Roy* (" Gosselin, Guardian of the Library of the King "). The Marquis D'O was a favorite of Henry III of France, was Keeper of the Royal Wardrobe, and also at one time Superintendent of Finances and Governor of Paris.

Gosselin apparently regarded the subject of scoring by fifteens in tennis as a serious one, for, after addressing "*Monsieur* O " under that nobleman's various titles, he begins his treatise with a philosophical dissertation on the body and the soul. He then proceeds to his main theme:

" Now thus it is (Monsieur) that in passing near a tennis court a short time ago I was seized with a fancy and desire to search for, and understand the reason why one counts (from time immemorial) in the game of tennis by fifteen, thirty, etc., and thus to know what those numbers of the game signify. I have been unable to find (a) man who could give me the reason for it. But after having thought of the matter intently at divers times I have finally solved the prob-

[72]

lem (found it) by my own reasoning (*mes solitaires discours*), and all the more *Monsieur* as I know that God has endowed you with various graces, among others great prudence and love for all things which depend on virtue and science: For this reason I make so bold as to present you with this research which I have made on the game of tennis, the knowledge of which is as rare as the game of tennis is common and general. I hope that your noble and excellent spirit will take great pleasure in hearing of this splendid and antique institution; all the more because the reason for it has with wisdom been found, and adapted for their use by the ancients, and has been unknown (as I judge) by the moderns up to the present."

Here we have then an astronomer, a mathematician, and a great scholar, with ready access to all the learning of France, informing us as long ago as 1579 that scoring by fifteens was ancient even in his time, and that he had never been able to find any one who could explain it. We find also Scaino, a great scholar, making the statement twenty-four years earlier that he had searched diligently, but been unable to find any literature ancient or modern on the subject.

It may be asked why we proceed farther in our inquiry. The answer is that tennis players of today, especially lawn-tennis players, who have had little opportunity to study the history of the earlier game, may be interested to consider some of the theories about the system of scoring expounded in remote places in the literature of different countries, and

hitherto difficult of access. We can at least have the satisfaction of knowing what we do not know, and some day,
out of the abyss of time, evidence may come to us that will
help solve the riddle.

The next two theories are expounded by Gosselin himself.
The first is the astronomical theory. Gosselin contends that
the numbers fifteen, thirty, forty-five, etc., could not have
been arbitrarily chosen, but must have been taken from some
definite measure, familiarly known to those who first practised the game. This measure is said to have been borrowed
from astronomy: A physical sign (or sextant) being the sixth
part of a circle, and itself consisting of sixty degrees, each
of which is divided into sixty minutes, and each minute into
sixty seconds, it seemed likely that scoring at tennis was imi-
tated from this division of the circle. For the physical sign =
four times fifteen degrees, as four times fifteen make a game
of tennis, and four games made a set, according to the practice in France at that date.

Gosselin then proceeds to treat this theory rather lightly,
contending that those engaged in striking and chasing a ball
were not likely to be students of the heavens. He then
expounds and approves what may be called the geometric
theory.

From a scale of measurements taken from the writings
of Varro, Pliny, and others, he maintains that the reason
for scoring as we do is derived from the *Clima*. Clima, he
explains, is a geometrical figure sixty feet square, or four

[74]

times fifteen feet in length and in breadth, making, like the game of tennis, four divisions of fifteen each.

These theories are repeated by Forbet, Sr. in 1599[5] and again by Hulpeau in 1632, when the rules or laws of tennis were printed in more complete form.[6] The modern theories then appear.

The chase line theory, expounded in 1885, is as follows:

". . . It may interest many of the players of lawn tennis how from that language (French) their mysterious system of marking has been derived. In all tennis-courts certain lines (called chases) are traced upon the floor; but on the service side they are in England only numbered up to six, and in France to fourteen inclusive. It is (speaking broadly) part of the marker's business to watch by what line the ball falls on the second bound, and call it out as the number of the 'chase.' If in the French court it falls by the number fourteen, he calls 'quatorze.' His next business is to call out also the strokes won by each player, four making a game. But he cannot call 'un' for the first stroke, because from 'un' to 'quatorze' inclusive means a chase. His stroke marking, therefore, begins at fifteen *quinze* as meaning one; and a stroke is even called 'un quinze' in France. 'Two' then becomes naturally 'trente'; three, 'quarante-cinq'; and the fourth stroke makes the game, unless the players stand at three strikes (or forty-five) each, when the scoring becomes

---

[5] Sevestre, T. *L'Utilité qui Provient du Jeu de la Paume.* Paris, 1599.
[6] Hulpeau, Charles. *Le Jeu Royal de la Paume.* Paris, 1632.

deuce, that is, *à deux* both equal — and to win the game either player must make two or three strokes running; or deuce-advantage — deuce-advantage — (advantage explains itself) may last for ever. The number of lines or chases in England is the same; but we presume that the Briton thought it saved trouble to number only the alternate lines up to six, and christen the rest by the mysterious style of one-and-two, five-and-six, and so forth. But in doing so he still retained what thereby becomes the utterly obscure 'fifteen' system of scoring, and made it worse by changing forty-five to forty, to save a syllable, and robbing his marking thereby even of the mildest arithmetical significance." [7]

This theory has been doubted because the scoring by fifteens existed long before chase lines were marked on the floor of the court. Chases may have existed, as they are mentioned by Gower about 1400, but apparently they were not marked out, the old custom being to have the marker put a mark on the floor where the ball stopped rolling or bounded a second time. There were no chase lines in Scaino's time, nor in 1632 when Hulpeau printed the book of rules. The earliest marking of chase lines in the court appears about 1719, between the time of Hulpeau and the time of Garsault. In a German work there is an old etching showing the chase lines marked out on the floor. [8]

---

[7] *New Book of Sports.* London, 1885. p. 84.
[8] Florinus, F. P. *Grossen Herren — Stands und Adelicher Haus-Vatter, etc.* Nuremberg, 1719. Vol. 2, pp. 894–5.

The next theory is that of the clock, expounded in 1913. It will be remembered that tennis existed in its early forms about the middle of the thirteenth century. During this period clocks dialed similar to those used today came into general use and were the subject of particular comment. This is the theory:

". . . Tennis scoring, like all other methods, must be based on some familiar or striking system of general calculation. We have already discussed the necessity of this, and have given instances. Now, when one looks about for some familiar mode of reckoning, in which the round total is sixty points, divisible into groups of fifteen, one naturally turns to the clock and the measurement of the hour. This is the only familiar system possessing the characteristics of tennis scoring. The hour of sixty minutes is divided on the clock face into twelve groups of five minutes each, three of which groups form a quarter of an hour. In early clocks, the hour was visually quartered, and the four groups of fifteen minutes apiece were thus emphasized. It is an exact parallel to the sixty points of the game at tennis, divided into four unitary groups of fifteen.

" On the face of it, it seems a plausible identification, far too exact to be a mere coincidence, and it is worth while to examine its claims in some detail. A game, we said, obtains its scoring from some familiar or striking general system of reckoning. Why, then, should not tennis have adopted the most familiar, that of counting by units? The answer is to assume that tennis was organized sufficiently to adopt a precise method of scoring, at an epoch when a familiar method of reckoning was improved by a striking development. The division of the day into twelve hours had been used from time immemorial, and the sun dial marked the division. But the invention of a mechanical clock, with its circular dial, was epoch making. It was an invention as striking and important as any in mediaeval times. It was already well developed by the thirteenth century. Saladin (to whose scientific countrymen the invention was due) gave an elaborate clock marking the seasons, the signs of the Zodiac, and the points of the compass, as well as the time of day and the hour, to the Emperor Frederick II in the thirteenth century. Three centuries before, weight clocks for striking the hour, not for marking time visually, were known. But by the beginning of the fourteenth century every cathedral possessed a modern clock. The invention had become part of civilization, and was still new enough to inspire interest and to suggest ideas. During its establishment the division of the hour into halves and quarters by the stroke of the bell became familiar. This was also visualized by the cross that quartered the dial. The climax, however, of the invention was the introduction of minutes and seconds, five minutes being marked in each interval between the hours on the dial, the familiar quarters being each fifteen minutes, and the hour, when ' the wheel had come full circle,' completing the tale of sixty minutes, thus divided, like the tennis game, into

[78]

four 'strokes' (of the bell), each accounting for fifteen 'points' of the minute hand." [9]

This theory is interesting and appears plausible, and it is disappointing to find that six years later the author throws some doubt on his own conclusions.

In 1920 Crawley propounded what we may call the coin theory:

" Now the sexagesimal system, whose origin is obscure, — it is older than Babylonian culture, whence it came to Graeco-Roman Europe, — was used in the Middle Ages not only by reckoning the hour, but also for money values, to a considerable extent. It must be understood that in this system the unit or standard was not 1, but 60; somewhat as the metre is now for measures. So in time-reckoning the unit was one hour (60 minutes), not one minute. Smaller numbers were expressed as fractions of the unit 60. This system was retained for the measurement of angles and for time-reckoning. But it was never the popular system; ordinary reckonings followed the Roman and Arabic systems of 1, 2, 3, &c. Another popular and primitive method was the division of any whole into halves and quarters.

" Tennis-scoring is, on the face of it, a sexagesimal system, to which is applied the primitive system of quartering a whole. The game, then, was the unit. The sexagesimal system was used and retained, along with others, in money, and predominated in the coinage of France between 1310 and

---

[9] Crawley, A. E. In: *The Field*. London, 1913. Vol. 122. pp. 301–302.

1410, according to actual records. We find a series of standard coins, variously styled, divisible into 60, and, especially in the century mentioned, quarters of this standard unit, value 15 each, the primitive quartering system being dominant over halving, probably through the influence of the Cross symbol, often stamped on the reverse. Actually, tradesmen were allowed to cut these coins in four pieces, and these were legal tender.

"Here are some typical specimens — in the time of Louis X (who curiously enough died from drinking cold water after a hard game of tennis in 1316) there was a *denier d'or à l'Agnel,* worth 15 sous; in 1340 we find the *double d'or,* worth 60 sous, in 1348 the *denier d'or à l'écu,* worth 15 sous, in 1411 the *couronne,* worth 15 sous. Even before 1310 we hear of *quinzains,* coins worth 15 sous. In modern French, *quinze* and *quinzaine* are used as we should say a 'dozen' or a 'score.'

"My suggestion, then, is that the scoring by fifteens, and by four fifteens to the game, originated in the convenient application of a unit coin value, 60 sous, which was worth four coins value 15 sous. It is a well-known fact that, in those days and for centuries after, tennis was practically always played for stakes. One of the earliest codes of laws for tennis contains three laws referring to stakes. Statutes of the realm are extant ordering tennis-stakes to be recoverable in the law courts. The money was placed under the *corde* (net), or more often entrusted to a third party. Kings and great men lost and won enormous sums. These were reckoned by the big coin, worth 60 sous, and generally known in the heyday of *paume* as *couronne* (crown). Thus the crowns painted in the tennis court may be given by humorists a double meaning, representing that the game of kings was not only played by crowned heads, but played for crowns. Naturally, the commonest big silver piece would be chosen as a convenient unit for the game; being worth 60 sous, each of its four parts was worth 15. And 15 was the value of each of the four strokes. Here, too, we have a simple explanation of the number of strokes, four.

"We noted that in the first mention of the system the author 'played for good stakes.' The present explanation is corroborated by the method mentioned by Scaino of reckoning a game of 4–1, or 4–2, as a single, 4–0 as a double, and 5–3 as a treble. Such valuation has no meaning whatever, unless (as in whist) the 'points' represented money." [10]

The above is the last contribution of a student of tennis, and a great theorist. After six years he wavers from the clock to the coin, having apparently devoted much time and money toward a solution of the problem.

This exhausts the various theories. Interesting as they are, we still lack absolute proof. One cannot help feeling that further research may throw new light on the subject, but until then we may have to rest on the statement made by so great an authority as Noel, who informs us as late as 1929 that

[10] *London Observer*. January, 18, 1920.

" the origin of the method (scoring by fifteens) and also of the English term 'love' to signify 'nothing' are mysteries." [11] It must be remembered that court tennis was played in its early forms long before the art of printing was invented, and that any new data must be found in old manuscripts that are difficult to discover, and often more difficult to decipher.

---

[11] Noel, E. B. *Tennis.* In: *National Review.* London, 1929. Vol. 92. p. 923.

Chapter VII

The Mystery of the Double Service

NO ONE appears to know how, why, or when two serves originated. The double service is an anomalous mystery, and a mysterious anomaly. Lawn tennis, squash tennis, racquets, and squash racquets copied the double service directly from court tennis, and again it is necessary to turn to the history of that game for information. There is little or nothing on the subject. Scaino, in his earliest work, does not mention the service, and other early writers are silent.

The character of early play with the hand and glove, the primitive battoir and racquet, was such that a severe service was impossible, and the serve may well have been considered relatively unimportant. In early days, the receiver was regarded as the attacking party, and the number of faults did not count. A server could keep serving without penalty until he put the ball within bounds.

An interesting survival of this early rule in court tennis is to be found in the " pass." If a ball served properly on the walls and pent-houses drops outside of the side-line of the receiver's court, it is a pass, and any number of passes are allowed today in England and France. This was formerly the rule in the United States, but today a pass is treated like any other fault where the service-ball drops outside the receiver's court; and only two are allowed.

Similarly, if a ball today is served in such a way that it even touches the very edge of the pent-house, it is a fault, but in Forbet's original rules of 1592, according to the tenth article, "it counted for nothing, unless, indeed, the players had agreed that every fault of every kind be counted against the striker." In other words, any number of such faults were allowed unless the rules were changed by mutual consent.

Other records confirm this view. In 1527, King Henry VIII paid a certain sum "to one that served the kinge's side at tennis at Hampton-Courte." The serve was regarded merely as a method of putting the ball in play, and could be made by an outsider.

In 1599, and again in 1634, the quotation occurs, "I ha been at tennis, madam, with the king. I gave him 15 and all his faults." This again shows how the service and faults were regarded. What scant evidence there is indicates clearly that the service was not considered of importance. This is the opinion of Marshall, who, after years of study, concludes:

"My own theory, however, which I express with diffidence, is that the service in those days (the days of Scaino, 1555) was a matter of small importance. Had it been otherwise, we surely should have had some mention of the conditions under which it was given or received, or of laws by which faults were defined.

"In the kindred and contemporaneous game of *pallone,* as we know, the service was given by a person who was an attendant, and certainly not otherwise engaged in the game."

Originally, therefore, the number of serves was unlimited. When it was reduced to two remains a mystery. Owing to the fact that the server with the hand, glove, battoir, or early racquet could not make a severe stroke, the serve may have been a handicap rather than an advantage.

But as racquets and balls were improved, the service became more and more important, until the wisdom of the double service began to be questioned. One service in lawn tennis was advocated in the press in England as far back as 1884. It has been agitated from time to time ever since. The agitation in the game of racquets became so strong, in the United States at least, that the double service has been eliminated, and the game much improved. There appears to be a growing sentiment in favor of one service in both lawn tennis and court tennis. Owing to the development of racquet and ball there is today too great a premium on the service. Both court tennis and lawn tennis have a tendency to become unbalanced.

In court tennis, the double service, and the inconsistent ruling that a ball does not have to be served beyond the service-line on the pent-house, have allowed two monsters to creep into the court, the " giraffe " and the " railroad."

These may be winning strokes, but they are awkward trick shots, and have no place in the game. Certainly it would be difficult to contend that there is any poetry of motion in them. They do not represent natural movements of the body, there is no lyric flow in their execution, and they mar the grace and beauty of the game.

Pierre Etchebaster, the professional court-tennis champion of the world, is undoubtedly the greatest player alive. Under the present rules of service, he has been able to defeat every opponent with comparative ease. His game is one of generalship, and is a model of accuracy, grace, and finesse. He believes that the game would be improved if only one service were allowed.[1] He believes also that a pass should be considered a fault, and that the service should properly strike beyond the service-line on the pent-house. He agrees with the writer that the allowance of two serves in lawn tennis is also a mistake, and that it tends to impair that game. The double service puts a premium on the hit-or-miss style of play, and takes away from its accuracy and finesse. The serve is an advantage, and it is an anomalous rule that allows two strokes to a player who has the advantage at the outset. It would be far more reasonable to allow two returns instead of two serves, if two strokes of any kind were to be allowed.

There is an old report, or it may be termed a bit of gossip, that one of the early kings who played tennis could not serve well, and that one day he made a rule that two serves should

---

[1] For Letter from Mr. Etchebaster, *vide Appendix*, p. 158.

be allowed. No one dared to object at the time, and no writer dared to publish any criticism later; thus, the rule stood unchallenged, and became part of the game. This is probably legendary, and no evidence has been found to substantiate it during the course of this search. It would appear to be contrary to the historic development of the service, which has been a limitation rather than an increase in the number of strokes. The tendency has been to decrease the number of services from an unlimited number to two, and if this tendency continues in the future there will be but one serve in both games. It is to be hoped that this change will take place. It would improve both games as much as it has improved the game of racquets.

Chapter VIII

The Origin of the Let

A STUDY of the service, especially in lawn tennis, naturally leads to a consideration of the let, because the
word *let* is most often applied to a service, otherwise good,
that touches the net. The word *let* means literally " obstruction." It is now almost obsolete, but appears in the current
expression " without let or hindrance." It is easy to see how
the word was used to apply to a ball that was hindered or
obstructed by a person or object in such a way that the point
had to be played over again. There is no such thing in court
tennis as a let due to the ball touching the net on the service,
because the player serves on the pent-house, and a service
ball cannot possibly hit the net. The word *let* first appeared
in the game of racquets about two years before lawn tennis
was introduced. The early rules of racquets provide:

" After the service, . . a ball hitting the gallery, netting,
post, or cushions in returning from the front wall is a let." [1]

Owing to the obstruction of the ball in its flight, it was
ruled in such a case that the point had to be played over
again.

---

[1] Stonehenge. *Rural Sports*. London, 1871. p. 635.

The rules in the first two editions of Wingfield in December, 1873, and November, 1874, make no mention of the let.

The first official rules of lawn tennis adopted by the Marylebone Cricket Club in 1875 provide that " it is a good service or return, although the ball touch the net or either of the posts." By 1878 the words " or either of the posts " were omitted, according to Jefferies' modern rules published in that year.

The first mention of a let in lawn tennis appears in 1878, where it is stated that a let should be allowed for outside obstruction or interference, such as " an obtrusive dog running across the court, or anything of that kind," but should not be allowed " for anything which constitutes a part of the court." [2] In other words, no let was allowed for a service that touched the net.

In 1880, however, the Marylebone Cricket Club and the All-England Croquet and Lawn Tennis Club definitely established the let in their decision that " if the ball served touch the net, the service, provided it be otherwise good, counts for nothing." [3] This rule was adopted in substance in the United States in 1881.

A great deal could be written on the philosophy of the let, and why a ball, otherwise good, that touches the net on the service is a let while a ball that touches the net on the return is not a let.

---

[2] Smythe, J. *Lawn Tennis*. London, 1878. p. 70.
[3] *The Field*. London, 1880. Vol. 55. p. 325.

Apparently it was thought, at some time during the development of lawn tennis, that two serves really gave too great an advantage to the server, and therefore a different rule was applied to a ball that was served than to a ball that was returned. It may have been an attempt to diminish the undue advantage to the server, which has persisted for so many years.

PLAYING OVER THE CORD
Early Form of Tennis
An Illustration by Hugh Thompson

Chapter IX

The Origin of the Net

THE NET did not originate in tennis, but undoubtedly existed long before the game was played. The word *net* is as old as the English language, and its derivation is uncertain. Nets were used for fishing as far back as there are any historic records. Erasmus, it will be remembered, advised, in 1524, leaving the net (*reticulum*) to the fishermen, and not to use the network of a racquet, but to play with the hand.

In early times, a simple cord was stretched across the court. This cord appears in the first authentic picture of a game of tennis, a painting formerly owned by the great historian, Julian Marshall. The full title of the painting is *David cum Barsabaea adulterio Uriam ab hostibus occidendum in praelium mittet,* and Marshall fixes the date as 1534. Similarly in the first book illustration in 1564, shown as the frontispiece, a simple cord divides the court. Hugh Thomson, in his illustration of the *Angler's Song* from Izaak Walton, portrays a plain cord. In Italy, for many years, a game was played by knocking a ball back and forth over a rope or cord stretched across an alley way or narrow street. The

Italian word for tennis, *palla della corda,* signifies a game that is played over a cord. There are streets in various towns in Tuscany named " via Della Corda," undoubtedly because the game was played in them.

Early in the seventeenth century it began to be the custom to attach tassels or fringes to the cord. These appear in the illustration of the first court in England, at Windsor Castle, and also in an artist's sketch in the writer's possession, that, according to experts, was drawn by the artist in the very early part of the seventeenth century.

It was not until about the middle of the eighteenth century, the time of Garsault, that the net was substituted and came into general use. Lawn tennis merely inherited the net from the earlier game.

PLAYING OVER THE FRINGED CORD. *Tennis in the* XVII *Century*
From Artist's Original Sketch

Chapter X

The Origin of the Ball

THE ORIGIN of the ball defies the historian because it antedates all history. The learned Antiquarius and Professor Gardiner go back in their researches about as far as history will permit, in tracing the origin of ball play, but throw little or no light on the origin of the ball.[1]

The balls used in court tennis were, in the oldest times, made of strips of cloth rolled together and stitched with thread. Later, for a period, they were made of leather stuffed with wool, feathers, bran, and other materials. In fact, some of the manufacturers in France began using inferior materials, so that in 1480 an ordinance was passed by Louis XI of France prohibiting the making of tennis balls except in a certain manner, and threatening confiscation of all those made in any other way. There was a time when it was quite popular to stuff tennis balls with human hair. Shakespeare, in his time, comments:

". . . the barber's man hath been seen with him; and the old ornament of his cheek hath already stuffed tennis-balls." [2]

---

[1] *Vide supra*, p. 98.
[2] Shakespeare, W. *Much Ado about Nothing.* Act III, Scene 2.

In 1920 there were found hidden in some of the dismantled rafters of Westminster Hall in London a few old leather-covered balls stuffed with hair. These were said to be hundreds of years old.[3]

The origin of our present type of lawn-tennis ball, however, can be definitely determined. It was invented by John Heathcote, one of the most famous of British sportsmen. An interesting account exists:

" In a very characteristic English country house there is preserved as an historical relic — it may become an heirloom — the first, the very first, covered lawn-tennis ball. It was invented within the family circle of Mr. John Heathcote, for very many years champion of real tennis, a great player and a great sportsman. When the new game was invented (in the early 'seventies) he found the uncovered ball over light, — to a player of the court game it must have felt light indeed, — and between the genius of himself and his wife the pattern of two globular strips of flannel, which would completely envelope a sphere, was worked out, and the flannel bandage applied. The invention was made public property." [4]

Various improvements in lawn-tennis balls have been made from time to time. The latest development is a seamless ball just coming on the market, and said to be better than anything yet made for play on hard courts.

---

[3] *Illustrated London News*. London, 1920. Vol. 157. p. 878.
[4] *Spectator*. London, 1926. Vol. 136. pp. 361–362.

Chapter XI

The Origin of the Racquet

WE HAVE seen how the racquet was adopted in tennis, and have traced its evolution since that time. It may have existed earlier than tennis, however, for its origin is remote, and not at all clear. The word itself is of uncertain etymology, and its derivation does not help us. Some maintain that it comes from the Arabic word *rahat*, meaning " palm of the hand " or " shaped like a palm." In such event it is very closely identified with tennis. Others maintain that it comes from the German verb *racken*, " to stretch," while others tell us it comes from the Latin *reticulum*, meaning literally " net." We find Erasmus, in his Latin dialogue on tennis, describing the racquet as *reticulum*, which may be translated " net-covered instrument." Nets had been used from time immemorial for fishing, and may well have suggested the idea of stringing for the various bats, battoirs, and other instruments for ball play.

If we regard a racquet as in substance an instrument strung with gut, for knocking a ball about in a game, we find it first mentioned in a Latin description of *chicane*. The translation reads:

"The young princes, separating into two equal bands, stationed themselves on horseback at each end of the arena. Thereupon, a ball made of leather, of the size of an apple, was thrown into the midst. Then the horsemen of both parties started at full speed, galloping towards the ball, and each holding in his hand a staff (*racquet*), long in proportion, and ending abruptly in a broad curvature, the middle of which was *divided-out* with gut-strings, dried gradually and plaited with one another, like a net." [1]

Chicane, which resembles lacrosse on horseback, was a very ancient game. Cinnamus, from whom the above quotation is taken, flourished from 1140 to 1185, so that the game undoubtedly was played prior to the middle of the twelfth century. The earliest games with racquets or similar implements were often played on horseback as well as on foot, especially in Persia, to which so many early games are traced.[2]

The actual beginnings of many games are impossible to prove, but a study of what is recorded gives the impression that most games played with a ball, and an implement to strike it with, had a comparatively simple and common origin. Let us consider first, by way of illustration, hockey, croquet, golf, and polo. We often hear the expression "by hook or by crook," little realizing the full richness of its meaning. We find, by tracing back, that hockey and croquet

[1] Cinnamus, J. *De Rebus Gestis.* Trajecti, 1652. pp. 186–187. For original Latin *vide Appendix,* p. 160.
[2] Antiquarius. In: *The Field.* London, 1927. Vol. 150. p. 740.

come from the French *hocquet* and *croquet,* both meaning
" a crook-stick." It is claimed that hockey was a shepherd's
game, probably introduced into England "from France
when pastoral dramas and pageants were in fashion, and
ladies and gentlemen dressed and accoutred themselves as
shepherds and shepherdesses." [3]

" The name of the game has been taken from the implement with which it is played, or, to speak more correctly,
with which the game in its rudest state used to be played,
the shepherd's crook. This was called in France a *croquet,*
and was simply a crook-stick. When and where it was
replaced with a mallet is unknown. Hockey, we have already said, is the French *hocquet* or *hoquet,* which, as well
as *croquet,* meant a shepherd's crook." [3]

Undoubtedly the expression "by hook or by crook"
meant with any kind of stick or "any old way," and so
came to have its present significance.

One scholar is quoted as stating:

" The first golfer was the medieval Scots shepherd, who
beguiled the weariness of watching his flocks on the St.
Andrews foreshore by hitting rounded white pebbles with
his crook into rabbit holes." [4]

The theory of the primitive shepherds knocking a ball or
other object about with a curved or knobbed stick seems
very plausible. They probably began with the flat side of the

[3] Prior, R. C. A. *Notes on Croquet: and Some Ancient Bat and Ball Games
Related to it.* London, 1872. pp. 15–50.
[4] *The Book of the Ball.* London, 1913. p. 34.

stick, this developing into our present games of golf and hockey.

An ancient Greek relief, and a fourteenth-century manuscript in the British Museum, illustrate a primitive game that would appear to be the predecessor of hockey and probably of golf.[5]

Sticks with heavier ends also were used, and these were developed into the polo mallet. Polo began in Persia, the land of the horse; passed into India, where it received its English name from the Thibetan word *pulu* or ball;[6] and was introduced from there into England in 1871.[7] Apparently another development came from the use of sticks with ends almost as broad as they were long, and this suggested striking with the end instead of the side, and gave rise to the croquet mallet. In early tennis, the players used a battoir or bat, which in essence was nothing else than another form of stick.

Stringing, however, was a new idea, and we find this first mentioned about the middle of the twelfth century. Apparently the game of *chicane,* already described, traveled into territories where the horse was not common, and at first it was played on foot, thus giving rise to a game similar to lacrosse.

However this may be, in many regions a game of ball is played on foot with implements of various kinds strung with

[5] Gardiner, E. N. *Athletics of the Ancient World.* Oxford, 1930. p. 214.
[6] Murray, J. A. H. *New English Dictionary.* Oxford, 1909. Vol. 7. p. 1081.
[7] *Encyclopaedia Britannica.* London, 1929. 14th ed. Vol. 18. p. 175.

ANETSÁ, CHEROKEE BALL PLAY IN GREAT SMOKY MOUNTAINS, 1930

gut. The games are so old that there is no way of proving in which country they began.

Lacrosse is very old, and may have had beginnings in different parts of the world at the same time. The history of our American Indians indicates clearly that it was played by them long before the landing of Columbus. The Canadians named it "lacrosse," the different Indian tribes using different names of their own. The Cherokee and Choctaw Indians also played the game, using "two small bats resembling tennis racquets." [8]

The Indian game is still played in the interior of the Great Smoky Mountains, a primitive region on the border of North Carolina and Tennessee. The Indians call it *anetsâ* (pronounced *ah-naay-tsaw*) and make the game an occasion for great celebrations. Their enthusiasm over it is as great as is ours over football, the ceremonies are more elaborate, the training more painstaking, and the game even more strenuous and violent.

An authority who dwelt in the "Great Smokies" for many years writes, in 1930:

"The Indian 'ball-play' . . . is still a favorite game of our Cherokees, who have not modified the original game in any respect. The teams fast, dance the livelong night before the game, sing or chant their ritual, are exhorted by the shaman and scarified by him, drink the magic herb-concoction, etc. You can see the game . . . in all its abo-

---

[8] *Encyclopaedia Britannica.* London, 1929, 14th ed. Vol. 13. p. 579.

riginal fierceness, with attendant gambling and hair-pulling
by the squaws, in some remote cove where the white officials
do not go.

" It seems to be the original of lacrosse; but the southern
tribes use two racquets instead of one." [9]

The Indians of the Great Smokies claim great antiquity
for their game, and it may literally be as old as their hills,
which were " old, very old, before the Alps, and the Andes,
the Rockies, and the Himalayas were molded into their
primal shapes." [10]

The problem of determining the very beginning of a ball
game, like lacrosse for example, is largely a problem of
language and written record.

Whatever older nations may claim, their historians, etymologists, and scientists, no matter what arguments may
be based on the derivation of words in ancient tongues,
the North American Indians have originated some of the
games that are played today. The origin of their games may
be as old, if not older, than the written records of any language, for there is nothing to prove the contrary. The more
one studies the games of the American Indian, the more one
becomes impressed with their great antiquity.

In an exhaustive compilation of Indian games for the
United States Government, the definite statement is made
that " there is no evidence that any of the games described

[9] Kephart, H., President State Literary and Historical Association of North
Carolina. March 29, 1930.

[10] Kephart, H. *Our Southern Highlanders*. New York, 1913. p. 52.

CHOCTAW INDIAN BALL PLAYER WITH RACQUETS
From *Catlin*, 1832

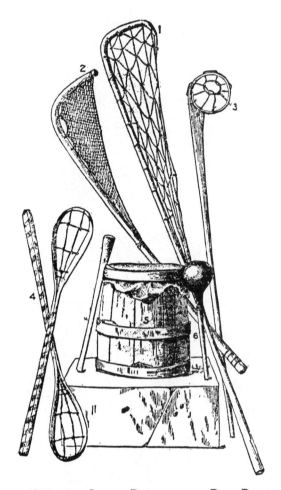

AMERICAN INDIAN RACQUETS FOR BALL PLAY

| 1 Iroquois | 3 Ojibwa | 5 Drum |
| 2 Passamaquoddy | 4 Cherokee | 6 Rattle |

were imported into America at any time either before or after the conquest." [11]

Let us consider the Indian ball play to which the Canadians gave the name of lacrosse. This was universal, not localized in any respect. The fact that every tribe in every part of the American continent played this game, and all claimed its great antiquity, is very impressive. As Mooney writes:

" The Indian game of ball play is common to all the tribes from Maine to California, and from the sunlit waters of the Gulf of Mexico to the frozen shores of Hudson Bay. When or where the Indian first obtained the game it is not our province to inquire, but we may safely assume that the brown-skinned savage shaped the pliant hickory staff with his knife and flint, and twisted the net of bear sinew ages before visions of the western world began to float through the brain of the Italian dreamer." [12]

A reference to the illustration showing the various types of racquets that have been used by the different tribes from time immemorial will assist us in forming our own conclusions.

---

[11] Culin, S. *Games of the North American Indians:* In: *United States Bureau of American Ethnology.* Annual Report 24. Washington, 1902–3. p. 32 and p. 563.
[12] Mooney, J. *The Cherokee Ball-Play.* Washington, 1890. p. 105.

MAJOR WINGFIELD'S RACQUET
1873–1874
First Lawn Tennis Racquet

1876 MODEL

1878 MODEL
Used until about 1883

1889 MODEL

1898 MODEL

1931 MODEL

EVOLUTION OF THE RACQUET IN LAWN TENNIS

Chapter XII

The Origin of Lawn Tennis

THERE is some controversy as to the evolution of lawn tennis but this much appears to emerge from the mass of conflicting opinions. Lawn tennis borrowed attributes from several different games. It is a happy medium drawn from widely divergent classes. It borrowed from royal tennis, from fashionable badminton, and from the lowly game of racquets. Racquets was actually a slum game until about 1832, when it was taken up at Eton and Harrow. In a note on the life of Sir William Hart Dyke, the first racquet champion, there is this extraordinary comment:

" It is said that until the time of Sir William's championship all those who successfully competed for the position of champion rackets player were either born or brought up in the debtor's prisons." [1]

The original racquet presented to William Gray in 1864 for winning the Irish Championship was obtained from his grandson by the writer, and placed among the trophies of The Racquet and Tennis Club of New York. This early racquet was made by the present well-known manufacturers,

[1] *British Sports and Sportsmen. Supra,* p. 417.

Messrs. Prosser & Company of London, and looks quite modern. It is in excellent condition, its stringing intact and unbroken, and its frame unwarped. It bears a close resemblance to the early lawn-tennis racquet of Major Wingfield of 1873–1874.

The next game to come into vogue was badminton, named after the Duke of Beaufort's seat in Gloucestershire, where apparently it was first played by the fashionables of the time. Originating in India, it was brought to England in 1873, shortly before lawn tennis was introduced.[2]

Badminton also influenced the size of the first lawn-tennis court, the height of the early net, and the first method of scoring, while court tennis influenced the later forms of racquet, the later type of net, and the final method of scoring.

It is interesting to note that early lawn-tennis sets were advertised as " Improved Wingless Tennis," probably to indicate that shuttlecocks were not employed as in badminton; and badminton was described as "the Anglo-Indian Game of Badminton or Lawn Rackets to distinguish it from the new game of lawn tennis." [3]

Crawley tersely sums up the result of years of study of its development:

" Being the only historian of the game who has worked out all the details of its origin, I make no apology for giving an account of this very interesting birth-process. The game

---

[2] *Encyclopaedia Britannica.* New York, 1929. 14th ed. Vol. 2. p. 917.
[3] Buchanan, J. *The Games of Lawn Tennis and Badminton.* London, 1876.

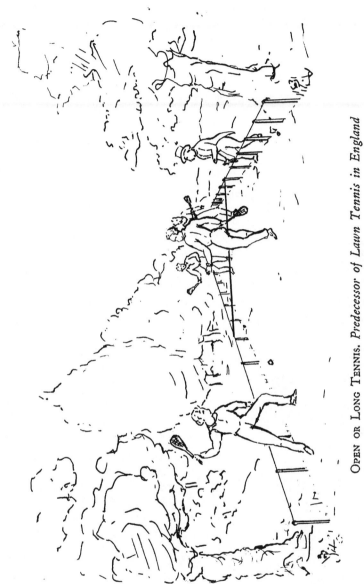

OPEN OR LONG TENNIS. *Predecessor of Lawn Tennis in England*

From Illustration of 1837

had several fathers, Major Wingfield, James Lillywhite, 'J. R. H. C.,' 'G. C. C.,' 'Major G. Perera,' and J. H. Hale, with Cavendish as its godfather, and three mothers — tennis, rackets and badminton." [4]

Lawn tennis was originally scored like racquets, and the court tennis method of scoring was not adopted until June, 1877, when the lawn-tennis committee of the All-England Croquet and Lawn Tennis Club adopted " tennis scoring by fifteens, games, and sets." [5] The rule was not adopted in the United States until the following year. According to the original score sheets of the Nahant tournament, the earliest tournament in America, the racquet method of scoring was used in 1876 and 1877, and the tennis or court-tennis method in 1878.

So much for the general evolution of lawn tennis. Is it possible to fix a date that may fairly be said to be the date of its origin? This depends largely on whether Major Walter Clopton Wingfield is to be given credit for having invented the game. Undoubtedly crude forms of a similar outdoor game were played before his time, and " open or long " tennis, shown in the illustration of 1837, represents one of them. For this reason, some of the correspondents of *The Field* in 1874 questioned his claim to originality. The consensus of opinion, however, is that he originated both the name and the game. In an excellent summary in the *Badminton*

---

[4] Crawley, A. E. *Technique of Lawn Tennis.* London, 1923. p. 8.
[5] *National Review.* London, 1922. Vol. 80. pp. 107–108.

Library, G. M. Heathcote comes to this very logical conclusion:

"For practical purposes it may be said that the epoch of lawn tennis dates from a no more distant period than 1874, when Major Wingfield resuscitated it by the introduction of Sphairistikè." [6]

In any event, on February 23, 1874, Major Wingfield applied for "letters patent . . . for the invention of a 'New and Improved Court for Playing the Ancient Game of Tennis,' and his claim to originality must have been recognized, for he was granted a patent on July 24, of the same year. *The Army and Navy Gazette,* in 1874, mentions the new game as a "clever adaptation of tennis (*i.e.* court tennis) to the exigencies of an ordinary lawn." Viscount Dunedin supports this view when he says:

"There can be little doubt that . . . the suggestion came from real tennis, — a game of great antiquity, — and that in lawn tennis there was a real invention." [7]

Lawn tennis began, therefore, as an invention embodying characteristics of different sports, tennis being the predominating influence. The game was born when the first rules were published. These rules or code of laws appear in the first edition of Wingfield's book, which is now available for study.

This is a small, eight-page pamphlet in splendid condition.

---

[6] *Tennis, Lawn Tennis, Racquets, Fives.* London, 1890. p. 132.
[7] *Fifty Years of Lawn Tennis in Scotland.* Edinburgh, 1927. p. 2.

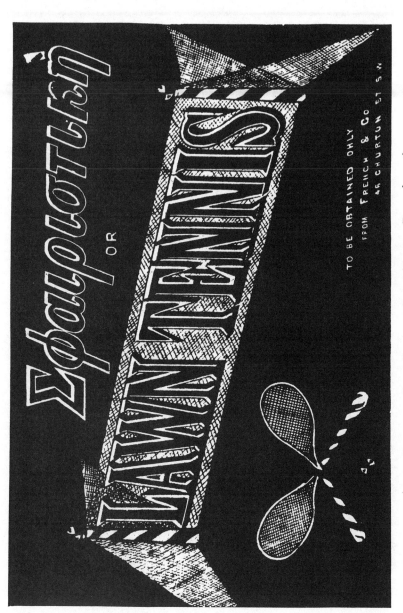

COVER DESIGN OF FIRST BOOK ON LAWN TENNIS. December, 1873

EARLIEST ILLUSTRATION OF A LAWN TENNIS COURT
England, 1873

On either side of its cover, in bright red letters, inscribed on a lawn-tennis net, is the imposing title, Σφαιριστικὴ, *or Lawn Tennis.* The title page reads:

THE MAJOR'S GAME

OF

LAWN TENNIS

DEDICATED TO

THE PARTY ASSEMBLED

AT

NANTCLWYD

IN

DECEMBER, 1873

BY

W. C. W.

LONDON:

Harrison and Sons, 59, Pall Mall

(Entered at Stationers' Hall)

It contains a picture of what may be regarded as the earliest lawn-tennis court.[8]

A description of the early type of court, and a most interesting prophecy, are given by Commander G. W. Hillyard of the Royal Navy:

" My earliest recollections of lawn tennis are somewhere about the middle 'seventies, when, on coming home from school one summer, I found that an uncle who was staying

---

[8] See Illustration opposite.

with us had marked out the lawn with a figure shaped like a gigantic hour-glass, with a net across what would be the waist of the glass. He told us it was a lawn-tennis court. The first we had ever seen. The net was about five feet high at the posts, and four feet or so at the centre. There was no centre tape, and the posts were not the heavy, firm ones of modern times, but thin, attenuated affairs with little flags stuck on the top, and held by guy ropes, which latter were always slipping, and constantly needing adjustment. The racquets were shaped very much like those used in tennis, heads heavily ' cast off ' and very small. My uncle appeared to think that there were great possibilities in the game, and prophesied a world-wide future for it." [9]

Commander Hillyard's memory is very exact, for, in one of the earliest books on lawn tennis printed in America, the description of the court corresponds very closely to that of the Commander:

" The posts are maintained in their positions in the same way as cricket nets — by guy ropes attached either to a hook or secured by holes in the posts to prevent their falling or yielding to gentle pressure . . . The net is attached to the posts at a height of five feet from the ground, and drops in the centre to a height of only four feet from the ground." [10]

According to a brief biography in *Who's Who*, Major

[9] Hillyard, G. W. *Forty Years of First-Class Lawn Tennis*. London, 1924. pp. 1–2.
[10] " Jefferies' " *Modern Rules of Lawn Tennis*. New York, 1878/9. p. 4.

Wingfield maintained until the day he died that he was "the inventor of lawn tennis." [11] If we grant his claim, and it seems to be well established, the next step is to determine when his book was first published. Here there has been confusion for many years, undoubtedly due to the fact that Wingfield did not apply for his Letters Patent until February 23, 1874, and the further fact that the greatest tennis historian, Julian Marshall, had noted on the Queen's Club copy, "First Edition, November, 1874, at earliest."

The first edition, described in detail in the Appendix, was published, however, in the preceding year. After the first edition appeared, the correspondents in *The Field* clamored for more adequate rules. Accordingly, on August 15, 1874, Wingfield wrote, "As I purpose bringing out a *new book* with revised rules, I shall be grateful for any help." [12] And he submitted a slightly revised court, showing for the first time both sides of the court marked out in the same way.

On November 28, 1874, in submitting his new rules, which had been expanded from the original six to twelve, Major Wingfield refers to "the above game (*Sphairistiké*, or *Lawn Tennis*) which I brought out at the end of last year." [13] He clearly refers to his original publication "at the end of last year," and it may therefore be concluded that lawn tennis originated in 1873, in all probability at the house

[11] *Who's Who.* London, 1911. p. 2115.
[12] *The Field.* London, 1874. Vol. 4. p. 172.
[13] *The Field.* London, 1874. Vol. 44. p. 590.

party at Nantclwyd in Wales. Since that time, the game has spread throughout the world. The interesting prophecy of Commander Hillyard's uncle in the early 'seventies has more than been fulfilled.

It is surprising, under the circumstances, that the historians have given so little information about Major Wingfield, especially as he was a man of commanding presence and personality, and came from one of the oldest and most distinguished families in England. The Wingfields were established in Wingfield Castle, in Suffolk, long before William the Conqueror came over from Normandy. Their historian proudly boasts that they were " a family always famous in its devotion to its king and country, which for more than eight hundred years has preserved an unbroken record of loyalty without a single stain on its escutcheon." [14]

It was in Wingfield Castle that Charles d'Orléans, the author of the first poem on tennis, was imprisoned. Charles had been captured by the English, and for many years was held a prisoner in various strongholds in England. Some of his jailors gave him little consideration, but in 1432 [15] he was transferred to Wingfield Castle, and put in charge of John Wingfield, who " was a cultured gentleman, a poet of sorts, and altogether capable of understanding his prisoner." [16]

Walter Clopton Wingfield was born in 1833, and was no

---

[14] Wingfield, J. M., Editor. *Some Records of the Wingfield Family*. London, 1925. Preface.
[15] Champion, P. *Vie de Charles d'Orléans* (1394–1465). Paris, 1911. p. 222.
[16] Orléans, C. d'. *Poésies*. Paris, 1923. Vol. I. p. 5.

Major WALTER CLOPTON WINGFIELD
Inventor of Lawn Tennis

exception to the splendid record of his family. In 1860, when he was twenty-seven years of age, he was put in command of a cavalry force during the campaign in China, and on his return to England he became Major in the Montgomery Yeomanry Cavalry. Later, he was one of the very select " Honourable Corps of Gentlemen at Arms, the Body Guard of the Sovereign at all Public and State Occasions." [17]

Wingfield possessed all the characteristics of the English country gentleman. He was an all-round sportsman, and athletic games were among his hobbies: tennis, racquets, badminton, cricket, and even croquet, that had arrived in England in 1856 and had become very popular by 1873.

But the Major wanted a more strenuous out-of-door game than those existing at the time. It was with the idea of obtaining such a game that he experimented on his own lawn with various adaptations.[18] He was familiar with the elements of many games, but tennis apparently was uppermost in his mind.[19] It was in this way he perfected his invention. He deserves great credit for his contribution to the health and happiness of many people in all parts of the world.

---

[17] *Hart's Annual Army List.* London, 1909. p. 130. 1911. p. 144.
[18] *Sunday Times.* London, July 1, 1928.
[19] *The Field.* London, 1874. Vol. 44. p. 220, 244.

Chapter XIII

The Origin of Lawn Tennis in America

THE ORIGIN of lawn tennis in America contains certain elements of mystery. The beginning is not entirely clear, there being different claims to the first court in the country. The reports have been inconsistent or contradictory, and no one appears to have marshaled the evidence of the different claims in an orderly or an impartial way. It is with the hope of clarifying the early history that a search has been made, and a survey of what has been found up to the present time is given.

The first claim of priority was that of a Miss Mary Ewing Outerbridge, who went to Bermuda in the Winter of 1874. There is a difference of opinion, mentioned later, as to whether " the Winter of 1874 " means the Winter of '73–'74 or the Winter of '74–'75. Miss Outerbridge had found a novel game called " lawn tennis " being played there by British officers attached to the regiment then resident in Bermuda. She had never seen the game before, and became so much interested that she persuaded the officers to let her have some racquets and a net, which she brought back with her in the Spring of the same year. On arrival at the port of New York, she had difficulty in getting her tennis set through the customs house, as no one knew what it was, and consequently could not classify it for duty.

Her brother, A. Emilius Outerbridge, was prominent in shipping circles, and she called upon him for assistance, and he helped her get the set through the customs. Mr. Outerbridge was an active cricketer and a director of the Staten Island Cricket and Baseball Club, which had its grounds at Camp Washington (later St. George), Staten Island. He obtained permission from the Club to allow his sister, shortly after her return from Bermuda, to set up her net and mark out a court in one corner of the grounds.

Another brother, Eugenius H. Outerbridge, now residing in New York, remembers distinctly his sister's first lawn-tennis equipment, especially the hour-glass shaped court. He recalls that she had a diagram indicating how the court should be laid out. Mr. Outerbridge, who was formerly Secretary of the Staten Island Cricket and Baseball Club, and at one time a member of the Executive Committee of the United States Lawn Tennis Association, wrote on August 2, 1923, to Dwight F. Davis, then President of the Association, that his sister's set was brought in from Bermuda in the Spring of 1874. This is the date according to all the traditions of his family. The set was generally regarded as the first one brought into the country, and no claim to an earlier set or an earlier court was made until later.

The earliest account yet found of Miss Outerbridge's

bringing the game to this country appeared in 1887 in an historical sketch of the Staten Island Cricket and Baseball Club:

"In 1875, Miss Mary Outerbridge, the sister of Messrs. A. E. and E. H. Outerbridge, having seen and played the new game in Bermuda, was so fascinated with it that she determined to equip herself with a complete tennis outfit, and, armed with a net, a set of rules, racquets and balls, she returned to America, and paid the U. S. customs duties on the first lawn tennis set ever brought into this country. She lost no time in interesting her friends in the pastime, and obtained a ready assent from the members of the club to erect a net on their grounds; for it must be remembered, that at this time the famous ladies' club had not come into existence.

". . . Miss Outerbridge was spending the winter of '74–'75 in Bermuda, and returned probably in the early Spring, when the exodus from the sunny shores of that charming winter resort generally takes place." [1]

In 1890, three years after this account, and about fifteen years after the event itself, an article by the first Champion of the United States, Richard D. Sears, was published to the effect that a court had been laid out in Nahant in August, 1874, and that this was the first court in this country:

" Judging from the interest taken in lawn tennis today in

---

[1] Clay, C. E. *The Staten Island Cricket and Baseball Club.* In: *Outing.* New York, 1887. Vol. 2. p. 104.

the United States, it seems hard to realize that fifteen years
ago the game was unknown there; yet it was the end of
August, in 1874, when the first set was laid out at Nahant,
a small seaside resort about ten miles from Boston. Dr. James
Dwight and Mr. F. R. Sears, jun., were the first two lawn
tennis players in America. . .

" It is rather a curious coincidence that another set was
imported the same autumn by Mr. Sherman of Newport, but
this was not set out until the following Spring.

" In the Spring of 1875, besides the set at Nahant, and the
one at Newport which has just been mentioned, there was
one at New York, and in the early Summer two more were
laid out at Newport. All of these sets were owned by private
people, and at that time none of the cricket or baseball clubs
had taken the game up. The set in New York was owned
by Mr. E. H. Outerbridge, who is today one of the Executive
Committee of the National Lawn Tennis Association of
America. Mr. Outerbridge obtained permission from The
Staten Island Cricket and Base-ball Club to lay this set out
in a corner of their grounds, and naturally this did more to
bring the game into prominence than anything else, as it was
the first set laid out in a more or less public place." [2]

This account, coming from such high authority, tended
to establish Nahant as the first scene of lawn tennis, and was
taken as the basis of many other reports.[3] Miss Mary Outer-

---

[2] Sears, R. D. In: *Tennis (Badminton Library)*. London, 1890. pp. 315–316.
[3] Slocum, H. W., Jr. *Lawn Tennis in Our Own Country*. 1890. pp. 106–108.
Paret, J. P. *Lawn Tennis*. New York, 1904. pp. 9–10. Lawrence, W. *Some Memo-*

bridge had died long before 1890, and this contention, after so many years had elapsed, was not regarded by the Outerbridge family as of sufficient interest or importance to question in any public way.

In the course of the present search, however, some information has been discovered that throws a different light on the subject. In 1891, in an illustrated article that appears to have escaped the historians, Dr. James Dwight himself makes this statement:

" The first set of lawn tennis in New England — indeed, I fancy, in the country — was played at Mr. William Appleton's place at Nahant. In the summer of 1875 a set of pharistiké (*sic*) or lawn tennis, was brought out from England, where the game was just coming into fashion. . .

" Mr. F. R. Sears, the elder brother of the champion, and I put up the net and tried the game. . .

" That is the first tennis that I know of that was played in New England, and for two years we played incessantly. At the end of our second Summer, in August, 1876, we held our first tournament." [4]

Seventeen years after this first article appeared, Dr. Dwight confirmed the date to Charles Willing, of Philadelphia, in a letter written on April 27, 1908, from Barnstable, Mass., in which he said:

---

ries of a Happy Life. Boston, 1926. p. 95. Wilson, F. A. *Some Annals of Nahant, Mass.* Boston, 1928. pp. 322–4.

[4] Dwight, J. *Lawn Tennis in New England.* In: *Outing.* New York, 1891. Vol. 18. pp. 157–60.

" To the best of my knowledge, the first set of Lawn Tennis was brought over to my uncle, Mr. Wm. Appleton, who had a place at Nahant, in July, 1875. We played there the last part of that Summer, and the next Summer, in September, we had our first tournament, using the racquet scoring. There were 15 entries.

" Mr. R. D. Sears was not old enough at that time to play. It was an older brother, Mr. F. R. Sears, who first played it with me. There was a larger tournament the next year, and one was held each year, as far as I can remember for a good many years. Of the first three, I am sure, as I have the records.

" The second set was, I believe, brought back from England by Mr. W. W. Sherman, and I played at his place at Newport in 1877 or '78.

" We played a great deal at the Powels', at the Boits', at both the Paran and Frederic Stevens', at Mr. Bennett's, etc., in Newport.

" You are quite welcome to use these facts for any article." [5]

On August 8, 1911, an interview with Dr. Dwight to the same tenor and effect was published in the *Evening Bulletin* of Philadelphia.

The exact year is fixed by reference to the tournament " in September of the next Summer," which the original score sheets clearly show was in 1876.

---

[5] Quotation from photostatic copy of letter; compare also Mr. Willing's article published in *Boston Evening Transcript*, Jan. 26, 1931.

These are the two principal claims to the earliest lawn-tennis court in this country, the only ones that so far have been supported by any form of evidence. Whatever conclusions may be drawn from the varying reports of these claims, there is no question but that the Outerbridge court was the first one in a public or semi-public place. This has been quite generally admitted.

The accounts, however, are inconsistent as to whether the private court at Nahant was laid out in August, 1874, or in the late Summer of 1875, and also as to whether the Staten Island court was laid out in the Spring of 1874 or in the Spring of 1875. In the light of what has been discovered, a review of the evidence will tend to clarify the history.

Dr. James Dwight, often called the " father of lawn tennis in America," was the first to play on the Nahant court. He is generally accredited with having laid it out, and his testimony is direct evidence. He has repeatedly stated that the Nahant court was laid out in the late Summer of 1875. No direct evidence to the contrary has been found, and the indirect evidence corroborates his testimony. For example, if the Nahant court, as reported in *Badminton,* was laid out in August, 1874, the Sherman court must have been established at Newport in 1875. But there is no evidence of such an early date. A notice in a New York weekly indicates 1876 as the first year at Newport; and Dr. Dwight himself did not play there until 1877.

Further substantiation of the year 1875 may be found in

the very description of the Nahant court. Dr. Dwight in his article states that " the service-line was 26 feet from the net." There was no such specification for the service-line until May 24, 1875, when the rules and regulations of the Marylebone Cricket Club were adopted. The little book described as the *Book of the Game,* that accompanied each early tennis set in 1873 and 1874, contained no such provision. The first edition of December, 1873, and the second edition of November 1, 1874, make no mention of any line " 26 feet from the net." In the third edition of June 1, 1875, however, there appear as specifications for the court the " Rules and Regulations, revised by the Tennis Committee of the M.C.C. 24th day of May, 1875, and published by their authority." These rules and regulations specify an hour-glass shaped court, 24 feet wide at the net, with base lines 30 feet wide, placed 39 feet from the net. We then find this provision: " Lines shall be marked out parallel to the net at a distance of 26 feet from it, which shall be called service-lines." There is a diagram with all the dimensions clearly indicated.

The Field published almost all references to tennis, but it makes no mention of a service-line " 26 feet from the net " until 1875. This data would clearly indicate that the Nahant court could not have been laid out in an earlier year. In all probability, the *Book of the Game* that accompanied the Nahant set was the 1875 edition of *Sphairistiké,* and the court was laid out according to its specifications.

So much for the Nahant story. In considering the Staten

Island story, other collateral information should also be borne in mind. The argument is often made that if Miss Outerbridge was in Bermuda in the Winter of 1874, she must have returned to New York "in the Spring of 1875." This, of course, depends entirely on what is meant by the Winter of 1874. The regular winter season in Bermuda is January, February, and March. Miss Outerbridge could well have been in Bermuda during January, February, or March of 1874, and returned to Staten Island during that period or later in the same year.

It has also been argued that tennis sets could not have arrived in Bermuda in the early months of 1874, because patents for the game were not applied for until February, 1874. It is true, as indicated in the Letters Patent themselves, that they were not applied for until February, 1874, but other records reveal that the original tennis sets were obtainable in 1873. The original book, the first edition, now in the writer's possession, was distributed in 1873. It is dated December, 1873, and states:

" This game has been tested practically at several country houses during the past few months, and has been found so full of interest and so great a success that it has been decided to bring it before the public, being protected by her Majesty's Royal Letters Patent." The original books, distributed with the tennis sets, advertised them for sale at five guineas each by " the inventor's agents, Messrs. French and Co., 46 Churton Street, London, S.W." There is nothing improbable,

SITE OF FIRST LAWN TENNIS COURT IN AMERICA
Camp Washington, now St. George, Staten Island

therefore, in some officer having taken the game to Bermuda in the early months of 1874, for it is quite common for British army officers to be the first to introduce new sports into the Colonies.

Miss Outerbridge, therefore, may well have obtained her lawn tennis set in Bermuda early in 1874, and brought it back with her to Staten Island in the same year. The early account of 1887, before any discussion of exact dates arose, would point to "the Spring of 1875," but other and later reports point to 1874. About twelve years ago Frank G. Menke, a well-known sports writer, stated in a newspaper article that the Outerbridge set was imported from Bermuda in 1874, and he repeats the statement in a book just published.[6] Mr. Menke maintains that his opinion is based on a published interview with a veteran customs inspector, since deceased, who was in the customs department at the time when the duty on Miss Outerbridge's set was assessed. This inspector, in a review of his career about the time of his retirement, asserted that the importation was made in 1874, and that he, as a customs agent, handled the first tennis apparatus ever seen in the United States. An examination of the records in the Customs House confirms this date. While the individual declarations of merchandise imported during 1874 and 1875 are no longer available, other official documents found there prove that Mary E. Outerbridge and her brother, A. E. Outerbridge, arrived in New York from

---

[6] Menke, Frank G. *All Sports Record Book*. New York, 1931. p. 184.

Hamilton, Bermuda, very early in 1874. The sailing list of the steamship *Canima,* shown in the illustration, and now published for the first time, establishes the date of her arrival. It settles beyond doubt a much mooted question, and confirms in every way the Outerbridge tradition.

The Nahant court, therefore, was not laid out until the late Summer of 1875, while the Outerbridge court was laid out in the early Spring of 1874. The historians have claimed two different dates for Nahant, but both are later than the Spring of 1874. The Outerbridge court at Camp Washington, now St. George, Staten Island, stands therefore as the earliest lawn-tennis court of any kind, public, semi-public, or private, in the United States. One of the earliest references to lawn tennis in the United States is in an illustration of the club grounds where the Outerbridge court was set up.

The very earliest reference is the sketch that appeared in the *New York Daily Graphic* on September 2, 1876. The illustration of the site of the Outerbridge court is a reproduction of an original sketch that was made on June 12, 1877, by a very distinguished cartoonist, who is alive today and has identified his work. He was on the staff of the *Graphic* at the time, and was requested to go and make sketches at Staten Island. It was the first time he had ever seen lawn tennis, and the event was regarded as one of considerable importance. His sketches were published in that paper on June 16, 1877, and the importance of the event is emphasized by an editorial that appeared in the same issue, containing

PASSENGERS' LIST.

T. W. Hoit & Co., Stationers and Printers, 61 WALL, N. Y.

District of New York, Port of New York.

I, John McKichan Master of the S.S. Canima do solemnly, sincerely and truly that the following List or Manifest, subscribed by me, and now delivered by me to the Collector of the Customs of the Collection District of New York, is a full and perfect list of all the passengers taken on board of the said S.S. Canima at Hamilton Bermuda from which port said S.S. Canima has now arrived; and that on said list is truly designated the age, the sex, and the occupation of each of said passengers, the part of the vessel occupied by each during the passage, the country to which each belongs, and also the country of which it is intended by each to become an inhabitant; and that said List or Manifest truly sets forth the number of said passengers who have died on said voyage, and the names and ages of those who died.

So help me God.

Sworn to this Feb 2 1874 John McKichan

John Waymouth S.S. Canima

John McKichan List or Manifest Of all the Passengers taken on board the S.S. Canima whereof

is Master, from Hamilton Bermuda burthen 419 tons.

| NAMES | AGE | | SEX | OCCUPATION | The country to which they severally belong. | The country in which they intend to become inhabitants. | Died on the voyage. | Part of the vessel occupied by each passenger during the voyage. |
	Years	Months						
Mary E Outerbridge	21		Female	Lady	United States	United States		Cabin
Emma Cleveland	42		"	"	"	"		"
Arthur H. Cleveland	9		Male	Minor	"	"		"
Annie Gomer	37		Female	Lady	"	"		"
Ino D Sargent	41		Male	Merchant	"	"		"
H A Curtis	54		"	Mariner	"	"		"
Aston Curtis	55		"	"	"	"		"
W G Watts	45		"	"	"	"		"
J L Platt	50		"	"	"	"		"
Stephen Bryant	57		"	"	"	"		"
Jane McParlin	26		"	"	"	"		"
A E Outerbridge	29		"	Merchant	Canada	Canada		"
W Mowe	38		"	"	Canada	United States		"
Dr F HolmesPass	46		"	Surgeon	United States	United States		"

10-3

FIRST LAWN TENNIS ILLUSTRATION PUBLISHED IN THE UNITED STATES
From *New York Daily Graphic*, September 2, 1876

a prophetic comment on athletics, especially with reference to women. This may be interesting for that reason to players of today who find tennis being played more and more by women in almost all countries:

Athletic Sports

" The *Graphic* to-day holds the mirror up to the face of the social world, and shows the new forms of recreation and enjoyment just coming into fashion. A quarter of a century ago gymnasiums for men were hardly thought of, and no such thing as a college gymnasium existed. Boat clubs, ball clubs and cricket clubs were rare, and these invigorating and exciting sports were looked upon with suspicion. There was no interest to speak of in athletic sports of any kind. But the movement had then begun, and has rapidly gained strength ever since, till every college in the country has not only its gymnasium, but its boat and other clubs, and athletic sports of all kinds are not only viewed with favor, but practiced with enthusiasm. Nor is the practice confined to young men. A few years ago the delightful game of croquet was welcomed by ladies, and soon became the fashion. It led the way to other out-of-door sports for ladies, and last week we reported the formation of an athletic club for the practice of archery and other field sports by ladies on Staten Island. The tendency is a good one, and ought to be heartily encouraged. These out-of-door exercises are as invigorating as they are enjoyable, and should be cultivated quite as much for physical development as for pleasure. Our people are fast relearning some of the old and forgotten truths of the Greeks and Romans and other ancient peoples. The care and culture of the body are essential to the full and free use of the mind and enjoyment of life, and there can never be a hardy and perfect race of men till women are properly developed and nurtured and trained. The physical side of life for women as well as for men, is beginning to receive the attention which is its due. A great deal has been written and said about physical exercise within twenty-five years, and heroic efforts have been made to get debilitated people to practice in gymnasiums. But it has been found that people will not take exercise alone if they can help it, any more than they will eat alone. The play of social instincts and affections adds as much to the benefit as it does to the pleasure of a dinner. Solitary eating is the next remove from fasting. To make physical exercise popular it must become a pastime. And athletic sports will become fashionable for ladies as well as for men in proportion as they are made sports, and ladies find pleasure in them. The sexes naturally go together, in joy as well as sorrow, in recreation as well as in toil, in play as well as in study and prayer. And the forms of exercise suited for both sexes will come into vogue, and many sports which a few years ago were considered unwomanly, will doubtless be fashionable. The coming woman is evidently determined not only to have culture and accomplishments, but a vigorous and healthy physical life. And athletic sports are the surest and pleasantest way of gaining this desirable result."

This is a remarkable prophecy. The changes that have taken place are very impressive, especially when we realize that the women of Japan and of Italy and other Latin countries have adopted the game.

Tennis has played and is playing an important part in the emancipation of women throughout the world, and they enjoy more freedom today than at any time in history.

Chapter XIV

The Catgut Mystery

EVERY BOY is told, when he begins to play lawn tennis, that his racquet is strung with catgut, and that he must not get it wet. Later he learns that racquets in almost all games are strung with the same material. He accepts the information without question, and as a matter of course. He knows that cats are sinewy and tough. They are tenacious of life. It is proverbial that they have nine lives. So — their guts ought to be as strong and lasting as any strings that could be found. This is not only the boys' belief, but is that of a great majority, old and young, based on a misapprehension that has persisted for more than a thousand years.

In 1929, at a tennis dinner in New York at which twenty leading tennis experts were gathered, the writer asked two questions: " What is catgut? " and " Why is it called catgut? " In the discussion that followed all said that when they were boys they thought catgut was made out of cats. A few knew what it was, but understood little of its use in modern manufacture. No one had the slightest idea of how it received its name. Here was an opportunity for another quest, a search that has wound its way back many centuries through the history of sport, then through the history of surgery, and finally through the history of music.

It may interest the players of today to know what catgut never has been, what it is, something of its use in the stringing of modern tennis racquets, and how it received its deceptive name.

To begin at the beginning, catgut has never had anything to do with cats, although such a belief has existed for many centuries. Catgut, whether used in tennis, in surgery, or in music, is made from the intestines of sheep. The authorities on the subject are all clear and in accord.

The word is " applied to cord of great toughness and tenacity, prepared from the intestines of sheep, or occasionally from the horse, the mule, or the ass. Those of the cat are not employed." [1] Rabelais, who wrote in 1533, tells us that the cords of court-tennis racquets in his time were " made of the guts of sheep or goats."

Now that the cat has been let out of the bag, so to speak, and we know what the material is, let us consider first its use in modern manufacture, and then the origin of the word. As a matter of fact, catgut is the heart of the lawn-tennis racquet. It comprises two-thirds of the total cost, and perhaps affects play more than any other one factor except the player's own efforts. The best tennis strings are produced from split gut that comes from the smooth side of sheep

---

[1] *Encyclopaedia Britannica.* New York, 1929. 14th ed. Vol. 5. p. 31. Also *Century Dictionary.* New York, 1913. Vol. 2. p. 861.

intestines or casings, as they are called. From the sheep's small intestine, which is more than twenty feet in length, there is taken an unbroken, narrow strip about as wide as one-third of the circumference. This strip is the thinnest, toughest, and smoothest part of the casing, and is known as the "smooth side." The other portion is known as the "rough side." It requires twenty-five or more of these strips, twisted together like a cable, to make one of the best quality fifteen-gauge strings, and two of these strings, one of nineteen feet and another of twenty-one feet, are required for each racquet. It takes, therefore, parts of fifty or more sheep to string one racquet of the best quality, a fact that is so little known that it may astonish even the well-informed tennis players throughout the world.

There are many tricks of the trade, of course, in gut manufacture, and much depends on skill and technique, as in any other industry. For example, the strings should be allowed to "age" for at least four months and preferably a year before being used. Unlike most animal substances, they grow stronger for a period, the tensile strength increasing from fifteen to twenty-five per cent in twelve months. Also the cleansing process should take place as soon as the sheep is slaughtered. If this is not done within twenty-four hours the gut begins to deteriorate and loses strength very rapidly.

But the raw material is perhaps the most important element. Some herds produce better gut than others. Climate and food are important factors. A careful and proper selection of this material is essential.

Other materials are also used. There is "oriental gut," produced in Japan and India. One- or two-foot sinews are taken from the legs and backs of cattle, and even from certain parts of whales, and these are combined with glue. The best stringing, however, is and always has been made from sheep.[2]

But, it may be asked, if sheep, mules, horses, cattle, asses, goats, and even whales have been used in the manufacture, why should the substance be called catgut? The history of sport throws no light on this question, so the history of surgery has been examined, because catgut is commonly used at the present time for sewing up wounds. References were found to " the stitching of wounds with a thread made from the intestines of sheep " a thousand years ago. While the medical works afford no answer, they do reveal two interesting facts that are worth comment: the Egyptians, thousands of years ago, used catgut for sewing up wounds. This surprised certain scholars, because they knew that the cat was sacred to the Egyptians. They were misled by the name, as people have been similarly misled for centuries ever since.

Some of the wounds sewn up with catgut did not heal. A belief became prevalent that there was something inherent

---

[2] From information obtained through courtesy of Walter L. Pate, of New York City.

in such an animal substance that caused suppuration. For this reason the surgical use of catgut was abandoned for centuries. It was not until 1869 that Lord Lister, the great English surgeon, discovered and demonstrated that it was the bacteria in the ligature, and not the ligature itself, that caused suppuration, and that if these were killed by antiseptic treatment there was no danger. Catgut was accordingly reintroduced into surgery, and still holds its important place in that science.

But why such a name? To find any satisfactory answer it was necessary to go back through the records of music almost to the realm of myth and legend. Many know that catgut is used for violins and other musical instruments, but few realize the great antiquity of its use for this purpose. Chappell says:

" From the time of the Homeric poems (*c* 1000 B.C.) to that of Terpander (which is supposed to have been about the middle of the seventh century before Christ), the lyre of the Greeks had but four strings. They were made of sheepgut, which is now technically called ' catgut.' While the number of strings was limited to four, the lyre must have been used rather as the substitute for a pitch-pipe to guide in the recitation of epic poetry than as a musical instrument. Nothing like tune could be played upon it, but still there would have been music in the Greek sense of the word since there was a combination of recitation, metre, and rhythm. In the Odyssey we read of a skilled singer and player on the lyre

(Phorminx) as having changed his chant to a new string
upon a new peg. . ."[3]

The literature of music is full of quaint references. The
violinist is mentioned as a " cat-gut-scraper " who "com-
mands at will the house of hospitality,"[4] and has been hu-
morously described as a man who " stretches the bowels of
a cat over a wooden box, and rubs them with the tail of a
horse."[5]

In early times, the bows were made of horse hair just as
they are today:

" As to the Romans, it is believed that the instrument
which they called ' cinnara ' was nothing more than a harp,
and its name only a translation of ' kynnor ' or ' kinnar,'
which in the Hebrew text of the Bible is the name of David's
harp. The number of strings to the ancient harp was originally 13, but this number was afterwards increased to 20 and
even to 40. These strings were made of catgut like those of
our harps, as appears from a Greek epigram in the An-
thology."[6]

" About the end of the eighteenth century a mechanic of
Milan, by the name of Gerli, introduced into several con-
certs and churches an instrument which had the form of
a harpsichord, and which was mounted with strings of

[3] Chappell, W. *Chappell's History of Music* (*Art & Science*). London,
1874. Vol. I. pp. 26–27.
[4] Wolcott, P. P. *Tristia*. In his *Works*. London, 1812. Vol. 5. p. 267.
[5] Heron-Allen, E. *Violin Making*. New York, 1885. pp. 208–209.
[6] Fetis, F. J. *History of Music or How to Understand and Enjoy its Performance*. London, 1846. p. 108.

catgut, played upon by bows of hair, according to the account given in the Italian journals of the time." [7]

In tracing the musical references the origin of the name was found. Catgut was originally called "kitgut." "Kit" was the old name for a small violin, and catgut meant at first "violin string" or "fiddle string." It has been explained on good authority that "the word is properly kitgut, kit meaning fiddle, and that the present form has arisen through confusion with kit-cat." [8] A prominent musician states that the cat is known to be peculiarly susceptible to the sound of the violin, and that he can play certain notes that will cause a cat to go into convulsions. This may have something to do with the origin of our expression "caterwauling," to which many humorous references are made in the history of music, but whether so or not, as far as the records disclose, the lamb and sheep have been led to the slaughter while the cat has remained inviolate throughout all the ages.

---

[7] *Supra*, p. 145.

[8] *Encyclopaedia Britannica*. New York, 1929. 14th ed. Vol. 5. p. 31. Also: *Century Dictionary*. New York, 1913. Vol. 2. p. 861.

EARLIEST MAGAZINE ILLUSTRATION OF LAWN TENNIS. From *Punch*, October 10, 1874

Chapter XV

The Influence of the Word Love

WHEN LAWN tennis was first introduced it was treated rather lightly by the masculine element. Apparently the Greek name *Sphairistiké* stirred up certain prejudices, and this may account for the fact that the name did not survive. In the press notices of 1874 many amusing comments appeared, some with a note of sarcasm.

One correspondent writes:

"I hear that Major Wingfield has made such a good thing out of the game, which has become astonishingly popular all over the world, that he intends bringing out an indoor game at Christmas with a Latin name, which will equal, if not surpass, its sesquipedalian Greek brother. The name, I understand, will not exceed ten syllables, and may be easily mastered in six lessons. If Major Wingfield can produce a really good indoor game — and I fancy he will — then I shall hail him as a benefactor of his species, as the very Archimedes of amusement."

It was regarded apparently as a very gentle game, suitable for the ladies. One writer remarks:

"I confess myself to a strong liking for croquet; but it has become too scientific now to please ordinary loungers of both sexes, who care only for something which will serve *pour passer le temps,* and enable them to enjoy fresh air and flirtation in agreeable combination."

Another describes it as "a game in which the delicacy and gentleness of a woman's touch counterbalances the mere strength of a man's arm, and provides an amusement in which both sexes can unrestrainedly share," and still another says, "It is far and away the best out-of-door game known. It far surpasses croquet or lawn billiards."

It will be remembered that an uncle in the early 'seventies showed the game to Commander G. W. Hillyard of the Royal Navy, predicting its great future. In referring to his visit the Commander says:

"I found great prejudice against it amongst my cricketing friends. They nearly all condemned it as fit only for women and quite unworthy of the attention of a man, certainly of a cricketer!" [1]

Why should the men of the time consider lawn tennis effeminate? Probably, in the beginning, this point of view was a direct inheritance from its predecessor, court tennis. There is a tale that is told in the ancient chronicles that illustrates this attitutde as long ago as 1414:

"On 27 February, 1414, at Kenilworth, the French am-

---

[1] Hillyard, G. W. *Forty Years of First Class Lawn Tennis*. London, 1924. pp. 2–3.

POPULAR IDEA OF LAWN TENNIS IN 1880
From *Punch's* Pocket Book

POPULARITY OF LAWN TENNIS IN 1880. From *Punch's* Pocket Book

bassadors derisively offered to send to Henry 'little balls to play with, and soft cushions to rest on, until what time he should grow to a man's strength.' Henry, though greatly angered, replied shortly: ' If God so wills and my life lasts, I will within a few months play such a game of ball in the Frenchman's streets that they shall lose their jest, and gain but grief for their game.' " [2]

Hall relates in early English:

" The Englishe Ambassadors, accordyng to their commission, required of the Frenche kyng to deliuer to the kyng of Englād the realme and croune of Fraunce with the entier Duchies of Aquitain, Normandy and Aniowe, with the countrees of Poytieu and Mayne and diuerse other requestes, offryng that if the Frenche kyng would without warre or effusion of Christen bloud rendre to the kyng their Master his uery righte and lawfull inheritaunce, that he would be content to take in mariage the lady Katheryn doughter to the Frenche kyng & to endewe her with all the duchie and countrees before rehersed. And if he entended not so to do, then the kyng of Englande did expresse and signifie to hym that with the ayd of God and help of his people he would recouer his right and inheritaunce wrongfully with holden with mortall warre and dent of sworde. The Frenchemen were much abasshed at these demaundes thinkyng theim very vnreasonable and farre excessiue, and yet not willyng to make any determinate aunswer till they had farther brethed

---

[2] Mowat, R. B. *Henry V*. Boston, 1920. p. 110. Quoting hitherto unpublished manuscript of Streeche.

[135]

in so weighty a cause, praied thenglishe Ambassadors to saie to the kyng their master that thei now hauyng no opportunitee to cōclude in so hie a matter would shortly send Ambassadors into England whiche should certefy & declare to the kyng their whole mynde, purpose and aunswer.

"The Englishe Ambassadors nothyng content with this doyng departed into Englande makyng relacion of euery thyng that was said or done. Here I ouerpasse howe some writers saie that the Dolphyn thinkyng kyng Henry to be geuen still to such plaies and light folies as he exercised & vsed before the tyme that he was exalted to the croune sent to hym a tunne of tennis balles to plaie with, as who said that he could better skil of tennis then of warre, and was more expert in light games then marciall pollicy. Whether he wer moued with this vnwise presente, or espiyng that the Frenchemen dalied and vaynely delayed his purpose and demaund, was moued and pricked forward I cannot iudge, but sure it is that after the returne of his Ambassadors, he beeyng of a haute courage and bold stomacke, liuyng now in the pleasantest tyme of his age, muche desiryng to enlarge and dilate his Empire and dominion determined fully to make warre in Fraunce." [8]

The story told in different ways is the source of Shakespeare's play of *King Henry V,* and, whether legendary or not, reveals how the game was regarded at that time. In

---

[8] Hall, E. *Hall's Chronicle* . . . carefully collated with the editions of 1548 and 1550. London, 1809. p. 57.

the play itself the King, on being presented with a barrel (tunne) of "tennis balls" by the Ambassadors from the Dauphin of France, replies in the tennis outburst so often quoted:

"We are glad the Dauphin is so pleasant with us;
    His present and your pains we thank you for:
    When we have match'd our rackets to these balls,
    We will in France, by God's grace, play a set
    Shall strike his father's crown into the hazard.
    Tell him he hath made a match with such a wrangler
    That all the courts of France will be disturb'd with chaces,
        etc." [4]

All down the years illustrations in *Punch* and other periodicals reveal the same attitude toward lawn tennis. In fact, a court-tennis player has treated lawn tennis with similar condescension. In 1891 a court-tennis enthusiast at Cambridge in his ecstasy wrote a prize poem with these comparisons:

"To see good tennis! What diviner joy
    Can fill our leisure or our minds employ,
    Not Sylvia's self is more supremely fair
    Than balls that hurtle through the conscious air . . .

    Let Cricketers await the tardy sun,
    Break one another's shins and call it fun;
    Let Scotia's Golfers through the affrighted land,
    With crooked knee and glaring eyeball stand;

---

[4] Shakespeare, W. *King Henry V*. Act I. Sc. II.

Let Football rowdies show their straining thews,
And tell their triumphs to a mud-stained muse;
Let india-rubber pellets dance on grass,
Where female arts the ruder sex surpass;
Let other people play at other things;
The King of Games is still the Game of Kings." [5]

This reminds the lawn-tennis player of the pot calling the kettle black, and adds insult to injury.

During the early days of lawn tennis in this country a similar attitude existed among the students of one of our great universities. On April 5, 1878, this letter appeared in the *Harvard Crimson:*

" Allow me a little space to expostulate, not ill-naturedly I hope, on a kind of athletics that seems to be gaining ground very fast at Harvard. I mean to say Lawn Tennis. There are now four clubs, and perhaps five, that have come into existence here this year. These clubs are generally composed of eight members each; that is, we have now at Harvard from thirty to forty men who devote their leisure hours to Lawn Tennis. Many of these men were formerly seen on the river, forming part of the club fours and sixes; now they have deserted these posts, where as much energy is needed as the College can supply, for a sport that will do themselves little physical good, and can never reflect any credit on the College. Is it not a pity that serious athletics should be set aside by able-bodied men for a game that is at best intended for a

---

[5] Stephens, J. K. In: *Cambridge Review.* May 19, 1891.

EARLIEST CARTOON OF LAWN TENNIS
From *Punch*, September 23, 1876

seaside pastime? The game is well enough for lazy or *weak* men, but men who have rowed or taken part in a nobler sport should blush to be seen playing Lawn Tennis." [6]

Why should such a point of view persist, and it did persist, and has persisted for centuries. Twenty years after the *Crimson* letter was written, winning an intercollegiate tennis match was not considered an athletic performance worthy of recognition. More than forty years elapsed before tennis players were honored with an " H " like other successful athletes. They were simply not regarded as athletes.

The attitude has been fostered by the word *love* exclaimed in scoring, which gave the general public an early impression that there was something languorous or love-sick in its form of exercise. The first cartoons in *Punch,* and many of the famous Du Maurier drawings, reveal the point of view even more clearly than early writings. " The new ground lawn-lords of England " were alluded to as " grasshoppers," and were cartooned accordingly.[7]

During the early 'nineties, when the tournaments were played at the Longwood Cricket Club in Brookline, Massachusetts, the younger element of the town used to gather by the fence along the highway to watch the play. They would often leave shouting in mocking tones, " Forty love." They mouthed the word " love " in extreme falsetto to indicate their supreme contempt for such an effeminate game.

---

[6] From original clipping of the *Crimson* obtained by courtesy of Dr. John W. Cummin of Boston.

[7] *New Book of Sports.* London, 1885. p. 81.

There is no question but that lawn tennis was regarded as a namby-pamby game until the late 'nineties, but even then it required great endurance, good condition, and stamina. A five-set match in the heat of summer was a severe test for any athlete. Frederick H. Hovey, a former champion of the United States, and a prominent college athlete during the 'nineties at Harvard, has given his opinion:

". . . As to the physical endurance and stamina required in lawn tennis, I have no hesitation in going on record as follows:

"As an old time letter man in football, baseball, hockey, track, and tennis, it is my opinion that a five-set tournament match of tennis in the heat of summer provides a greater test of physical endurance and stamina than does a similar contest in any of the other athletic sports."[8]

Other well-known athletes have expressed the same opinion; among them the late Robert D. Wrenn, former United States Champion, and also a great athlete, excelling as well in football and hockey, both regarded as very strenuous games.

But perhaps the most persuasive testimony is that of the late Eustace H. Miles. He was a well-known writer on athletic sports, and an authority on physical training. While he was a good lawn-tennis player, he was a master of court tennis and racquets, winning the championship of England in both these games. It is natural for a player to favor the

---

[8] Extract from letter of Frederick H. Hovey, February 4, 1930.

difficulties of games at which he excels, and yet Miles has expressed the opinion that lawn tennis is the most violent, because the player must always *go to the ball,* whereas in games like court tennis and racquets, which have side walls and a back wall, he may often by skilful playing wait for the ball to come to him.[9] He has said: "Personally, I find lawn tennis by far the hardest and most scientific of all ball games that I have tried." [10]

Popular opinion has changed during the past fifty years, and it continues to change even at the present time. It is a measure of progress.

---

[9] Paret, J. P. *Lawn Tennis.* New York, 1904. Preface.
[10] Miles, E. H. *Lessons in Lawn Tennis.* London, 1899. p. 13.

Chapter XVI

Tennis in the Life of Tomorrow

WHATEVER CHANGES may have been wrought in human nature by civilization, the Great War demonstrated that man's fighting instinct has not been subdued, that he must still find expression for his energy, and satisfy his desire for combat. In the early days, society, broadly speaking, was divided into the military and the non-military classes. Physical training was favored by the military classes because it fitted men to carry arms, but was opposed by many among the non-military classes, especially the ecclesiastics in control of education. Such an exaltation of the temporal flesh instead of the immortal mind was viewed askance. David sang his LI *Psalm,* and religious zealots for centuries taught that man was actually conceived in sin and shapen in iniquity. Their followers were inspired to mortify the flesh, to impair rather than to perfect the form and motion of the body.[1]

Gradually and unconsciously this attitude has changed. Some of the forgotten truths of ancient culture have crept into our consciousness. The belief has grown that proper exercise will quicken and purify the mind, as well as develop and strengthen the body. The care and culture of the

---

[1] For similar prejudice against the human body among the philosophers, *cf.* Lippmann, W. *A Preface to Morals,* New York, 1930, p. 155. *Appendix* p. 160.

body have become more and more a part of our philosophy of living. Under the hurried conditions of modern life those who devote some of their time to regular exercise, competitive enough to be diverting, gain a respite from the nervous tension of work, and acquire a poise and reserve force that helps them through periods of strain and trial.

More recently the idea has been developed that if war is to be avoided there must be substitutes for some of its functions. As William James says in his well-known essay:[2]

" So long as anti-militarists propose no substitute for war's disciplinary function, no *moral equivalent* . . . they fail to realize the full inwardness of the situation. . . So far war has been the only force that can discipline a whole community, and until an equivalent discipline is organized I believe that war must have its way."

Another writer states: " An all-wise Providence has provided that man's instinctive tendencies must be either expressed, repressed, or sublimated," that the fighting instinct and the keenness for combat " is innate, part of the soul and substance of every normal man, as much as and even more so than the love of truth and beauty," and he proposes " organized sport " as a " substitute for war of something whose appeal is as universal as war."[3]

These may be Utopian ideas, but militarists as well as

---

2 James, W. *The Moral Equivalent of War, New York Association of International Conciliation, 1910.* (International Conciliation Leaflet No. 27.)

3 Jessup, E. C. *The Sublimation of War Through Sport.* In: *Princeton Alumni Weekly,* Princeton, 1924, Vol. 25. pp. 249–250.

pacifists must admit that the tendency of sport is away from quarreling, and is in the right direction. Sport and military training have many similarities. " Be a sport " and " Be a soldier " mean about the same thing.

Sport provides discipline, self-control, and elements of exercise that are found in war, and at the same time it satisfies man's innate love of combat and competition.

Tennis in particular fulfills many of the necessary requirements, and it is interesting to note that its terms are in essence those of warfare: " volley," " kill," " cut," " stroke," and " smash " are military terms.

Sport had its early beginnings in France. The word *sport,* spelt originally *disport,* comes from *desporte,* the earlier French word. In the latter part of the sixteenth century and the early part of the seventeenth, tennis was played everywhere throughout the country. Sir Robert Dallington, British Ambassador, in describing France in 1598 informs us:

" As for the exercise of Tennis play, which I above remembered, it is more here used than in all Christendom besides; whereof may witness the infinite number of Tennis Courts throughout the land, insomuch as yee cannot finde that little Burgade, or towne in France, that hath not one or more of them. Here are, as you see, threescore in Orleans, and I know not how many hundred there be in Paris: but of this I am sure, that if there were in other places the like proportion ye should have two Tennis Courts for every one Church through France. Me thinks it is also strange, how apt they be here to play well, that ye would thinke they were borne with Rackets in their hands, even the children themselves manage them so well, and some of their women also, as we observed at Blois.

"There is this one great abuse in this exercise, that the magistrates do suffer every poore Citizen and Artificer to play thereat, who spendeth that on the Holyday, at Tennis, which hee got the whole weeke for the keeping of his poore family. A thing more hurtfull than our Ale-houses in England, though the one and the other be bad ynough. And of this I dare assure you, that of this sort of poore people, there be more Tennis Players in France than Ale-drinkers, or malt-wormers (as they call them), with us." [4]

Tennis flourished in France until the reigns of Louis XIV and Louis XV, when, with other athletic contests, it fell into disfavor. Most of the tennis courts during this period were abandoned or used for other purposes. The age of fastidiousness, extreme delicacy and languor, the age of Fragonard and Watteau, considered tennis too violent. De Luze describes in a humorous vein the former decadence of the game in his own country:

"It is without doubt a change due . . . to the way of living and of dressing, which has caused the decadence of the athletic sports of ancient France, and if we have to sum up in a word the cause of this decadence we say it is the wig

---

[4] Dallington, Sir R. *A Method for Trauell. Shewed by Taking the View of France. As It Stood in the Year of Our Lord 1598.* London, c. 1605.

which gave the signal for it. Today, by a curious contradiction in history, sport has taken its revenge. If woman has cut off her hair and shortened her skirts, it is sport which is responsible (whether it is called tennis, golf, or automobile) and sport, to tell the truth, is not a passing fashion but a necessity. . ." [5]

As we have seen, England for a time considered tennis as effeminate, while France regarded it as too strenuous. During recent times, however, the points of view in the two countries have converged, and today both the English and the French regard the game as an ideal form of athletics.

Ambassador Jusserand is largely responsible for reawakening the spirit of sport among the French. In a review of his splendid book on the sports and games of ancient France, Elizabeth Lecky, the wife of a great historian, describes his influence:

" The problem of an education which best equips a man for the battle of life is growing ever more perplexing. ' Art is long and time is fleeting.' As the number of subjects increases, the task of keeping the right proportion among them becomes more difficult. To each nation the problem presents itself differently. When we travel through England on a holiday we are struck at every turn by the cheerful sight of fields where men and boys play football, cricket, and other games. Not so in France, where the old love of sports has

---

[5] Luze, A. de, *Le Jeu de Paume, Jeu National Français.* In: *La Revue de Paris.* Paris, 1930. Année 37. T. 6. p. 364.

languished since the eighteenth century, and especially since the Napoleonic wars. There is now a movement in England, if not to supersede these games by rifle and drill, at least to encroach on the time given to them. No doubt the training of a man for the defense of his country should be now, as it was in the old days, one of the objects of education, and it is not likely that the military ardor we have witnessed (since the Peace Conference) will greatly modify tastes that have become part of the life and character of the people. If it did it would be a national misfortune, for no one will deny that England owes some of her greatness to the qualities that are fostered by these games, such as energy, self-confidence, self-control, healthiness of body and mind, and that spirit of good-fellowship which makes even enemies friends over a game of cricket or football. In France, thoughtful men are fully alive to the fact that outdoor games have a large and beneficial share in the formation of character, and they are doing what they can to revive them in face of the prejudice and criticisms of those who consider such a movement anti-national. M. Jusserand's book, by showing that some of the current sports have a French origin, may do much to overcome such prejudices. His epilogue is an eloquent protest against the general indifference to physical education in France, and an earnest endeavor to stir up his countrymen, by showing its importance." [6]

---

[6] Lecky, E. *Sports and Games of Ancient France.* In: *Longman's Magazine.* London, 1902. Vol. 40. pp. 117-129.

This comment portrays clearly the English point of view toward sport and athletics in general. It is a viewpoint that has been steadfast, dignified, and consistent for centuries. Owing to international games and friendly rivalry of different nations in sport, it is a point of view that is spreading throughout the world. If we are prepared to accept it, tennis will more than hold its own, and the future of the game will be assured. The early form, court tennis, provides an ideal exercise for those of more mature years who have to spend much of their time in cities, while the later form, lawn tennis, is ideal for the young who have free opportunity to play in the out-of-doors.

In a recent symposium on the subject, there is this tribute to lawn tennis:

" The general public is beginning to realize that there is more sustained action in tennis than in any other outdoor exercises, such as baseball, football, golf, or cricket. It requires better physical condition and more endurance than any other sport, with the possible exception of swimming. . . . A tennis bout is as personal an encounter as a ring contest or a duel with swords. Punch, skill, control, speed, stamina, head, and heart decide the issue. It's a sportsman's pastime and a fighter's game." [7]

The energy of youth must find expression. It is as inconsistent to preach restraint to the young without providing an

---

[7] Wingate Memorial Lectures. *Intimate Talks by Great Coaches.* New York, 1930. p. 256.

outlet for their energies, as it is to preach asceticism on a diet
of rare viands and rich wines.

" God gave the house of a brute to the soul of a man,
    And the man said ' Am I your debtor? '
    And God answered ' Make it as clean as you can,
    And then I'll give you a better.' "

This is a good, simple philosophy for us all. We should
care for our bodies so that we will be proud rather than
ashamed of them. We shall all be happier when the idea
that the body is the source of iniquity is relegated to the
Dark Ages, and we recognize it as the tabernacle of the soul,
something with a sacred element to care for and make a
visible expression of the mind and spirit.

This point of view is fostered by sport, and tennis has
become a universal sport among the nations. A " king of
games and a game of kings," " a sportsman's pastime and
a fighter's game," tennis will surely continue to play an even
greater part in the life of tomorrow than it has played in
the past.

Appendix

Page 20. THE FIRST BOOK ON LAWN TENNIS

	FIRST EDITION No date	SECOND EDITION 1st November 1874 (In back of book)	THIRD EDITION 1st June 1875 (In back of book)
Inside Cover	(No Page Corresponding)	The Game of Sphairistike	The Game of Sphairistike or Lawn Tennis Third Edition 1875
Title Page	The Majors Game or Lawn Tennis dedicated to The Party Assembled at Nantclwyd in December 1873 by W. C. W. (Printed)	The Game of Sphairistike dedicated to the Party Assembled at Nantclwyd in December 1873 by (Portrait of author without hat or tennis racquet) Walter Wingfield (Signature)	The Game of Sphairistike dedicated to the Party Assembled at Nantclwyd in December 1873 by (Portrait of author with hat and tennis racquet) Walter Wingfield (Signature)
Total Numbered Pages	8	38	45
Numbered Pages of Text	8	17	24
Number of Rules	6	12	25
Press Notices	None	9	12
Complimentary Letter	None	Letter March 11, 1874	Letter March 11, 1874
Illustration of Court	*with service crease and man serving*	*without service crease and woman serving. Differs from First Edition in many details*	*Identical with illustration in second edition*

Page 20. THE FIRST BOOK ON LAWN TENNIS (*continued*)

	FIRST EDITION	SECOND EDITION	THIRD EDITION
Obtainable from	Messrs. French & Co., 46 Charlton St., London, S. W.	Messrs. French & Co., 46 Charlton St. Pimlico London, S. W. and A. & J. Tompkins Tennis & Racket Courts, Brighton	Virtually same as second edition but in different form
List of Purchasers	None	"In testimony of the excellence of this popular game the inventor calls attention to the following list of titled personages who have recently bought it 1st November 1874." (naming) 124 Personages	Same as second edition but naming "Distinguished Personages" 1st June 1875 140 Personages 4 Clubs Life Guards Royal Horse Guards Numerous Regiments Eton, Oxford, Cambridge and various colleges and schools.

[*Note*] SINCE obtaining my copy of *Sphairistikè* or *Lawn Tennis* and preparing the material for this book, I have become convinced by a careful examination that a copy now owned by Miss Elizabeth Dwight of Boston, daughter of the late Dr. James Dwight, is also a copy of the first edition.

My copy, therefore, and Miss Elizabeth Dwight's copy are the only copies extant so far as known, although other copies may appear after this book is published. Attention is called to the means of distinguishing between the different editions.

M. D. W.

Page 22. Chart showing Various Spellings and Foreign
  Equivalents

THE word tennis has been written with four variations of five letters;
twelve variations of six letters; seven variations of seven letters, and
one variation of eight letters, or in twenty-four different ways in all:

5 *letters*	6 *letters*	7 *letters*	8 *letters*
tenys	tennys	tennyse	tennysse
tenez	tenetz		
tenes	tennes		
tynes	tenyse		
	tenyce		
	teneys		
	tenyys		
	tinnis	tinnies	
	teneis	tinneis	
	tenice	tennice	
	tenise	tenisse	
	tennis	tennies	
		tennise	

The word for tennis in other languages:
jeu de paume (*French*)
ballspiel
ballenspiel } (*German*)
katzenspiel
katspel (*Dutch*)
kaelspel (*Flemish*)
cach
catchpel } (*Scotch*)
caitch
juego de pelota (*Spanish*)
jugar al blé (*Basque*)

Page 26. VELLUTI, DONATO. CRONICA DE FIRENZE d'all anno M.CCC in circa fino all M.CCC.LXX Firenze, 1731

TOMMASO DI LIPPACCIO fu cherico benefiziato oltr' a' monti , bello della persona , e grande , ardito come un leone ; vendè il detto benefizio , e tornossi di quà , essendoci venuti 500. cavalieri Franceschi , che fu della bella , e buona gente vidi mai , e aveano grande soldo , tutti gentiluomini , e grandi Baroni , tra' quali vidi uno , ch' era maggiore tutto il capo , e collo , che niuno grande uomo , e 'l piè lungo più di mezzo braccio , e quasi tutti furono morti nella sconfitta di Altopascio ; giucava tutto il dì alla palla con loro , e di quello tempo sì cominciò di quà a giucare a tenes , (p. 34). Photostatic copy of original in possession of Malcolm D. Whitman.

Page 28. MINSHEU, JOHN. Ductor in Linguas, The Guide into the Tongues. London, 1617

11502 Tennis *play*, of τείνω Græc: *i. to stretch out*, aut à *tenéz* Gal: *i.hould*, which word the *Frenchmen*, the onely tennis players, *vse to speake when they strike the ball, at tennis*. G. Le ieu de la paúlme, *quod antiquitùs* palma manus *ludebant*. I. *Giuóco della pálla*, i. jocasi pila. H. Iuégo de la pelóta. P. *Iógo da bola, ô peli*. L. Sphæromáchia, à Gr. Σφαιζομαχία, pilæ, lusoriæ certamen, à σφαῖζα, i. pila quæ in sphæristerio lúditur, & μαχέομαι, i. pugno, *quasi* pugna pilaris, *pugna illa qua certatur pila*. B. Kaetspel, à kaetse, *i. ictus, percussio & speel, i. ludus, lusus*, Ball-spiel, *a* ball, *i. pila & spiel, i. lusus*. T. Ballenspyl, idem. Br. *Ye chwarepel*.

b *a* Tennis *court*. G. Tripot. L. Sphæristerium, ij. Gr. Σφαιρισήριον, à σφαιρίξειν, i. pila ludere. B. Kaetsbaene, *locus quo pila luditur, pro ceteris*. Vid. Tennis *play, in* Tennis *supra* (p. 486).

Page 46. CELLINI, BENVENUTO. (1500–1571). La vita di Benvenuto Cellini seguita dai Trattati dell' Oreficeria e della Scultura e dagli Scritti sull' arte. Prefazione e note di Arturo John Rusconi e A. Valeri. Roma: Societá Editrice Nazionale, 1901

Avevo in questo mio castello un giuoco di palla da giucare alla corda del quale io traevo assai utile mentre che io lo facevo esercitare. Era in detto luogo alcune piccole stanzette dove abitava diversa sorte di uomini, in fra i quali era uno stampatore molto valente di libri: questo teneva quasi tutta la sua bottega drento nel mio castello, e fu quello che stampò quel primo bel libro di medicina a messer Guido.

TRANSLATION (*Nugent*)

My castle had a tennis court, from which I derived great benefit; at the same time that I used it for exercise, there were many habitations in it, occupied by several men of different trades, amongst whom there was an excellent printer: almost his whole shop was within the precincts of my castle, and it was he that first printed the excellent medical treatise published by Signor Guido.

Di questo giuoco della palla si parla anche nell'atto o privilegio con cui Francesco I donò al CELLINI il piccolo Nello. — Dicevasi *giocare a corda*, o *alla palla a corda,* per ragione della funicella che tiravasi in alto a una mezza altezza, e divideva per metà lo spazio del giuoco per la sua lunghezza, come si usa anche oggi; e in varie città di Toscana le strade dove si giocava presero il nome di *Via Pallacorda.*

TRANSLATION (*Nugent*)

This game of tennis is mentioned also in the deed of concession by which Francis I gave the little Nello to Cellini. It was called the game of the cord or the game of the ball and cord, on account of the small rope which was set at medium height dividing in half the length of the court as is done now-a-days; and in several cities of Tuscany the streets where this game was played took the name *Via Palla Corda.*

Page 48, 66. The First Poem on Tennis

J'ay tant joué avecques Aage
A la paulme que maintenant
J'ay quarante cinq; sur bon gage
Nous jouons, non pas pour neant.
Assez me sens fort et puissant
De garder mon jeu jusqu'a cy,
Ne je ne crains riens que Soussy.

Car Soussy tant me descourage
De jouer, et va estouppant
Les cops que fiers a l'avantage.
Trop seurement est rachassant;
Fortune si lui est aidant:
Mais Espoir est mon bon amy,
Ne je ne crains rien que Soussy.

Vieillesse de douleur enrage
De ce que le jeu dure tant,
Et dit, en son felon langage,
Que les chasses dorenavant
Merchera, pour m'estre nuisant;
Mais ne m'en chault, je la deffy,
Ne je ne crains riens que Soussy.

Se Bon Eur me tient convenant,
Je ne doubte, ne tant ne quant,
Tout mon adversaire party,
Ne je ne crains riens que Soussy.

CHARLES D'ORLEANS

Page 86. Letter from M. Pierre Etchebaster

Maplewood, le 20 Juillet, 1931

Monsieur MALCOLM D. WHITMAN
261, Fifth Avenue, New York
Monsieur Whitman:

Je suis très flatté d'être sollicité par vous, pour vous donner mon impression sur le régime des deux balles de service dans les jeux de lawn-tennis et court tennis.

Cette question déja m'a beaucoup interressé, car je suis opposé au régîme actuel.

La loi d'une balle me paraîtrait aider et embellir encore davantage les jeux de lawn et court tennis.

Il me semble qu'au régîme actuel, c'est-á-dire avec les deux balles, le plus grand bénéficie d'un net avantage; cette réserve d'une seconde balle pousse le serveur á donner un service si rapide qu'elle lui enleve trop souvent malheureusement toute sa beauté et finesse. Nous assistons fréquement aussi á des parties, où la victoire sourit plus-tôt au meilleur serveur plus-tôt qu'au joueur plus complet en jeu.

En court tennis particulièrement, nous aurions avec une balle au service la suppression du service " Railroad," ou du moins la possibilité de le voir atténuer.

Bref, avec une " seule balle au service" mon impression est que les jeux serait plus attrayant, plus beau, tout en ayant plus de finesse et que nous assisterions à des parties où la victoire irait tourjours au meilleur.

Je souhaite, M. Whitman, que votre publication apporte dans le sein des Fedérations de lawn et court tennis le motif de conversations au point du vue de ce changement.

Veuillez croire, M. Whitman, à mes sentiments les meilleurs, et tout mon dévouement,

(*Signed*) PIERRE ETCHEBASTER

APPENDIX

Mr. WHITMAN:

I am much flattered to be requested by you to give you my impression of the rule of two service balls in the games of lawn tennis and court tennis.

This question already has interested me very much, for I am opposed to the custom. The rule of one ball would appear to me to improve and embellish the games of lawn and court tennis.

It seems to me that the custom of allowing two balls gives the server too decided an advantage; this reservation of a second serve encourages the server to give such a swift serve that it takes away too often unfortunately all its beauty and finesse. We frequently attend matches where victory smiles on the best server rather than on the best all-round player.

In court tennis particularly we would have with one service ball the suppression of the "railroad" service, or at least the possibility of seeing it lessened in importance.

In short, with a "single service ball," my impression is that the game will be more attractive, more beautiful, even having more finesse, and that we would attend matches where victory would always go to the best player.

I hope, Mr. Whitman, that your publication introduces to lawn and court tennis clubs the *motif* of our discussions so that this change may be put into effect.

Believe, Mr. Whitman, in my best wishes and sincere regard,

(*Signed*) PIERRE ETCHEBASTER

Page 96. The First Mention of a Racquet

Cinnamus, J. *De Rebus Gestis.* Trajecti, 1652

Juvenes aliquot æquo inter se numero divifi, factam ex corio pilam, magnitudine autem malo fimilem, in loco quodam, ad id prius dimenfo defcriptoque, fublimem jaciunt, atque ad eam, velut præmium in medio pofitam, plenis inter fe habenis contendunt: finguli in dextris virgam habentes, mediocriter longam, fed mox in orbem invurvatam ibique fidibus paulum diftantibus, cæterum retis in modum inter fe connexis, diftentam (p. 186–187).

Page 142. Lippmann, W. A. A Preface to Morals, New York, 1930 (page 155).

"There is no doubt that, in one form or another, Socrates and Buddha, Jesus and St. Paul, Plotinus and Spinoza, taught that the good life is impossible without asceticism, that without renunciation of many ordinary appetites no man can really live well. Prejudice against the human body, and a tendency to be disgusted with its habits, a contempt for the ordinary concerns of daily experience is to be found in all of them, and it is not 'surprising that men, living in an age of moral confusion like that associated with the name of the good Queen Victoria, should have come to believe that if only they covered up their passions they had conquered them. It was a rather ludicrous mistake, as the satirists of the anti-Victorian era have so copiously pointed out."

Index to Text

A

Advantage, the term: 68, 69, 76
Aldington, Richard: 63
Alexander III: 44, 45
Alfonso I: 67
Allemagne, H. R. d', quoted: 46
All-England Croquet and Lawn Tennis
 Club: 89, 105
Altopascio, battle of: 26, 27
America, *see* United States, the
Antiquarius, quoted: 35, 93, 96
Appleton, William: 116, 117
Arabia: 29
Archery: 47
Ariston of Carystius: 34
Army and Navy Gazette, The, quoted:
 106
Athenaeum, quoted: 25
Austria, *Archduke* of: 49, 50, 67

B

Backgammon: 55
Badminton: 103, 104, 105, 111
Badminton, quoted: 118
Bailey, N., quoted: 64
Ball, lawn-tennis, invention of, 94
Ball, tennis: 29–32, 44, 93, 94, 96
Baseball: 61, 115, 140, 148
Battoir, *see* Racquet
Beaufort, *Duke* of: 104
Bel, Philippe le: 44, 46
Bennett, *Mr.*: 117
Bibliothèque Nationale: 71
Blackfriars Monastery: 47

Blazy, E., quoted: 70
Boits, the: 117
Bonde, la: 46; *see also* Tennis
Book of the Game, see Sphairistiké
Borzia, Lucrezia: 67
Boston, Mass.: 12, 55
Bowling: 47
Box, C., quoted: 60
British Sports and Sportsmen, quoted:
 43, 50, 103
Brodie, M. K., quoted: 60
Brooks, Henry Mortimer: 17
Brundusium, Italy: 34
Buchanan, J., quoted: 104
Butler, Samuel, quoted: 64

C

Carystius: 34
Castiglione, Baldassare, *Count*, quoted:
 50, 51
Castile, *King* of: 49, 50, 67
Catgut: 126–132; oriental: 129
Cavendish: 105
Cellini, Benvenuto, quoted: 41, 46, 156
Century Dictionary, quoted: 127, 132
C., G. C.: 105
Champion, P., quoted: 110
Chappell, W., quoted: 130, 131
Charles V: 46
Charles IX: 71
Chase lines: 75, 76
Chaucer: 47
Chicane: 36, 95, 96, 98
Cinnamus, J., quoted: 96, 159
C., J. R. H.: 105